MATH WORKBOOK

for

Personal Financial Literacy

Editor in Chief: Donna Battista
Acquisitions Editor: Katie Rowland
Editorial Project Manager: Emily Biberger
Managing Editor: Jeff Holcomb
Associate Production Project Manager: Alison Eusden
Senior Manufacturing Buyer: Carol Melville
Cover Designer: Stephanie Lindsey
Full-Service Project Management and Composition: Gillian Hall

5 17

PEARSON

PearsonSchool.com/Advanced

ISBN 10: 0-13-216757-3
ISBN 13: 978-0-13-216757-4

PREFACE

The *Math Workbook* consists of problems and applications to help you hone and practice your personal finance math skills.

Each chapter begins with a discussion of a mathematical concept and how it relates to personal finance. The discussion is followed by three sections of problems to answer:

- **Math Review** is a series of math drills.
- **Apply Your Knowledge** asks you to apply the concepts you practiced to personal finance problems. The icon placed next to this section indicates that these problems are available on MyFinLitLab. MyFinLitLab
- **Open Response** exercises require you to compute the answer and explain the answer you get. The problems relate to personal finance topics discussed within the textbook, such as financial planning, insurance, and loans.

Two other topics, mortgages and supply and demand, are also discussed in the appendices of this workbook.

CONTENTS

Basic Financial Math

Money and math go hand in hand. Creating budgets, making investments, and deciding which car to buy all involve mathematics. Evaluating retirement options and calculating house and car payments also involve math. In fact, you will see that there are many very practical applications for mathematics in your life. Math is a tool we can use to our advantage, and in this workbook we'll show you how and where to use this tool.

You will find there are many times in your everyday life that you will need to add, subtract, multiply, or divide. You might be at the flea market or a garage sale and need to add up your items to know how much you owe. You may decide that the total is too much, so you will need to subtract items. At the store, you might buy multiples of one item and need to multiply the item price to figure the total amount. You might want to buy only one of an item that is on sale at "3 for $1.99," so you must divide to calculate the cost.

How about percentages? Why do you need to work with these? What if you went shopping and found a pair of jeans on sale for 25 percent off? If the price was originally $45.99—how much will you pay for them at the register?

This first chapter includes problems that will have you using these basic arithmetic skills in everyday situations. The chapter is divided into sections that provide review of simple problems. After you have completed all the reviews, you will find word problems, and then two open response problems.

Name: ______________________

Date: ______________________

CHAPTER 1

Basic Financial Math

CONCEPT #1: Adding Whole Numbers

2	7	5	6	3
6	9	2	9	1
3	4	1	8	7
+ 9	+ 5	+ 6	+ 7	+ 6

12	34	14	55	17
25	4	63	4	27
36	56	86	23	61
10	67	90	98	5
+ 54	+ 22	+ 7	+ 3	+ 90

133	7	10	94	5
369	541	531	613	678
54	422	7	5	43
753	41	935	834	567
5	976	153	168	970
+ 459	+ 104	+ 66	+ 99	+ 412

1,122	7	7,955	486	463
4,123	43	456	56	4
512	352	1,532	3,645	7,881
6	5,274	45	2	973
9,587	689	6,317	7,535	66
88	7,345	8,452	956	2,145
+ 671	+ 345	+ 9,656	+ 84	+ 3,561

10,877	45,987	24,587	2,357	54,783
5,406	245	27	4,588	234
65	87	8,457	950	25,156
751	12,345	4,575	751	68,567
9,450	459	25,785	45,774	567
84	74,564	674	39,302	68
6	5,845	49,587	481	95,778
+ 21,587	+ 89,727	+ 34,785	+ 354	+ 56,789

43 + 4 = ________	654 + 31 + 87 = ________	4,578 + 524 = ________
65 + 9 = ________	871 + 52 + 31 = ________	8,412 + 658 = ________
99 + 3 = ________	311 + 81 + 45 = ________	3,115 + 214 = ________

MyFinLitLab **Apply Your Knowledge**

1. Jeremy mowed three yards this week and charged $25 for the first one, $35 for the second one, and $50 for the biggest yard. How much did he make this week mowing yards?

2. Natalie's grandmother gave her $50 for her birthday. She also received gifts of $45, $25, and $30 from her three aunts. How much did she get for her birthday?

3. Lakita sold three shirts at a yard sale for $2 each and four pairs of jeans for $3 each. How much did she make in the yard sale?

4. Belinda paid $6 for a personal pan pizza, bought a tee shirt for $16, and a soft drink for $1. How much did she spend in total?

5. Dara had to pay $50 in band fees, $25 for the school club fee, and $30 for a lab fee. How much money does she need to cover her fees?

Name: ____________________

Date: ____________________

CHAPTER 1

Basic Financial Math

CONCEPT #2: Subtracting Whole Numbers

99 – 65	48 – 7	24 – 3	98 – 66	36 – 12
456 – 88	616 – 13	975 – 31	374 – 43	765 – 57
1,587 – 742	5,875 – 87	3,451 – 45	9,874 – 1,851	4,578 – 346
12,756 – 31	35,267 – 645	76,512 – 9,018	24,132 – 3,746	61,524 – 10,918

56 – 31 = ______	5,341 – 235 = ______	2,344 – 36 – 91 = ______
65 – 26 = ______	1,452 – 511 = ______	3,521 – 44 – 101 = ______
89 – 52 = ______	3,389 – 652 = ______	1,249 – 68 – 436 = ______

MyFinLitLab **Apply Your Knowledge**

1. Hal's dad owes him $100 for helping him clean out the barn. However, Hal borrowed $20 from his dad last week and $14 the week before that. How much will Hal's dad owe him after subtracting those debts?

2. Neela has an account balance of $432 in her checking account. She just wrote checks for $31 and $22. How much will she have in her account when those checks clear the bank?

3. Balia took in $4,221 with his yard-care business last year. However, he also spent $320 on gasoline and bought a used lawnmower for $400. How much did he make after deducting his expenses?

4. James has $1,000 in his savings account. How much will he have left after spending $555 on a used motorcycle and $120 for a good helmet?

5. Karla's income tax refund was $1,120. How much will she have left after paying her mother the $322 she owes her and buying a new calculator for $125?

Name: ____________________

Date: ____________________

CHAPTER 1

Basic Financial Math

CONCEPT #3: Multiplying Whole Numbers

12 × 4	61 × 6	25 × 9	11 × 8	52 × 7
243 × 11	311 × 18	561 × 22	741 × 62	112 × 15
8,753 × 345	4,537 × 856	7,112 × 487	6,541 × 521	8,511 × 214
41,526 × 32	97,468 × 41	51,241 × 11	87,994 × 56	77,556 × 24
9,827 × 53	8,524 × 61	7,638 × 82	5,423 × 95	8,258 × 77
156,235 × 13	9,861 × 437	347 × 578	47,834 × 4,573	35 × 57

55 × 67 = ______ 4 × 24 × 12 = ______ 123 × 98 = ______

15 × 71 = ______ 6 × 13 × 27 = ______ 431 × 65 = ______

43 × 21 = ______ 3 × 41 × 62 = ______ 367 × 41 = ______

MyFinLitLab **Apply Your Knowledge**

1. If Jordan drives an average of 11,234 miles a year, how many miles will she have on her car in seven years?

2. Brantley receives an average of $110 a year for his birthday. Ignoring any interest income he might receive on his money, how much money will he accumulate over a five year period?

3. Jeremiah wants to set aside enough money for lunch during the coming year. How much money will he need to save assuming he eats four days a week for 32 weeks and spends $3 per lunch?

4. Jose bought seven shirts for an average of $12 each and five pair of jeans for an average of $32 each. How much did he spend in total for his clothes?

5. Kelsey anticipates making about $55 a night in tips by waiting tables during the coming 12 weeks. How much will she earn in tips?

Name: ____________

Date: ____________

Basic Financial Math

CONCEPT #4: Dividing Whole Numbers

54 ÷ 3	68 ÷ 16	111 ÷ 8	1,122 ÷ 51	12,137 ÷ 53
110 ÷ 10	153 ÷ 17	434 ÷ 31	2,604 ÷ 56	23,616 ÷ 123
95 ÷ 5	252 ÷ 56	698 ÷ 4	3,125 ÷ 125	17,952 ÷ 68
48 ÷ 6	255 ÷ 15	567 ÷ 42	5,698 ÷ 14	51,562 ÷ 16
16 ÷ 4	162 ÷ 9	636 ÷ 12	9,526 ÷ 11	66,349 ÷ 1,543

66 ÷ 3 = ______ 184 ÷ 46 = ______ 9,841.5 ÷ 243 = ______

98 ÷ 4 = ______ 629 ÷ 37 = ______ 7,701 ÷ 453 = ______

65 ÷ 5 = ______ 121 ÷ 11 = ______ 4,650 ÷ 155 = ______

MyFinLitLab **Apply Your Knowledge**

1. Jermaine paid $300 for five concert tickets for himself and four friends. How much does each of his four friends owe him for his ticket?

2. Garth traveled 360 miles and used 12 gallons of gasoline. How many miles per gallon did he get?

3. Brianne paid $30 including the tip for the meal. How much did it cost each girl if there were a total of five girls that ate?

4. Basil paid $60 on his meal card at school. How much will each meal cost him if the card paid for 12 meals?

5. Senka charged $120 on her credit card to buy everyone in her group a T-shirt. How much did each shirt cost if she bought eight shirts?

Name: ____________________

Date: ____________________

Basic Financial Math

CONCEPT #5: Decimals

64.57	112.23	456.63	692.34	45.53
253.10	78.15	12.15	87.14	473.16
8.65	1,159.36	269.87	6,193.51	1.52
+ 7,845.43	+ 564.30	+ 5,421.83	+ 7.24	+ 5,524.61

45.87	786.31	1,125.32	489.63	65.21
− 33.12	− 562.14	− 698.31	− 15.98	− 23.56

554.97	556.59	111.26	55.23	128.79
× 45.10	× 62.55	× 82.36	× 14.02	× 51.11

534.86	34.12	1,432.43	89.41	12,445.32
÷ 87	÷ 4	÷ 65	÷ 32	÷ 98

66.12 + 31.45 + 115.78 = ________

231.25 + 61.21 + 578.59 = ________

569.32 − 58.98 = ________

125.31 − 72.54 = ________

452.69 − 53.76 = ________

42.11 × 15.25 = ________

79.58 × 6 = ________

2,255.31 × 35.81 = ________

362.15 ÷ 52.11 = ________

41.25 ÷ 3 = ________

1,875.80 ÷ 4.52 = ________

MyFinLitLab **Apply Your Knowledge**

1. Aisha paid $33.15 for the pizza for her and her two friends. How much did it cost each of them for the pizza?

2. DeMarcus bought a T-shirt for $20.87 and put $45.75 worth of gas in his car. How much did he spend today?

3. Jillian sold 12 shirts for $9.85 each. How much was her total sales?

4. Debbie had $347.32 in her checking account. How much does she have now after writing a check for $23.87?

5. Ranoldo spent $5.87, $7.32, and $6.41 on lunch this week. How much did he spend in total for lunch?

Name: ____________________

Date: ____________________

Basic Financial Math

CONCEPT #6: Percentages

Converting decimals into percentages:

0.25	______	0.33	______	0.64	______	0.98	______
2.50	______	0.42	______	0.75	______	1.10	______
1.23	______	0.61	______	0.47	______	0.11	______

You may find it necessary to calculate a percentage in a different manner. For example, 15 is what percent of 75? In this case you simply divide 15 by 75 or 15 ÷ 75 = .20 or 20 percent. Work the following similar problems.

8 is what percent of 32? ______________

5 is what percent of 100? ______________

11 is what percent of 66? ______________

17 is what percent of 111? ______________

28 is what percent of 30? ______________

110 is what percent of 365? ______________

52 is what percent of 321? ______________

12 is what percent of 75? ______________

MyFinLitLab **Apply Your Knowledge**

1. Talik was looking at a video game that was priced at $35.88. However, he also knows that sales taxes are 8 percent of the total and will be added to the price. How much will the sales tax be on this purchase?

2. Jeleeza got a 5 percent raise from her boss. If she was making $8 an hour, how much is she making now?

3. Gasoline prices are expected to increase by 22 percent next year. If gas is currently selling for $3.75 a gallon, how much do you expect it to be next year?

4. Belinda saw that food prices increased by 11 percent in the past two years. How much would $100 worth of groceries purchased two years ago cost today?

5. Guya paid 20 percent more for a name-brand entertainment system than a generic one would have cost him. Assuming the generic system was $400, how much did he pay for his home-entertainment system?

Name: ______________________

Date: ______________________

Basic Financial Math

OPEN RESPONSE #1

Please answer all parts of the question in the space provided.

Prompt: Sasha wants to go to the department store this Saturday for the big sale. She has saved $45, received $75 from birthday gift cards, and will receive $125 on Friday from work. Her mother reminds Sasha of the $39 she owes her for the last pair of jeans. Sasha also needs to put $50 in her savings. The sale has $40 jeans at 20 percent off and T-shirts on sale for 3 for $15.99.

1. How much money does Sasha have to spend? Show or explain how you got your answer.

2. How many pairs of jeans and T-shirts can Sasha purchase? Show or explain how you got your answer.

Scoring Guide

4 Student gives correct answers for parts 1 and 2. All explanations are clear and complete. There is evidence of clear understanding of the concept.

3 Student gives correct answers for parts 1 and 2. Explanations are correct, but possibly unclear. There is less evidence of clear understanding.

2 Student answers 1 (1 or 2) part of the questions completely correct. There is some evidence of understanding.

1 Student gives only parts of correct answers. There is little evidence of understanding.

0 Response is totally incorrect or irrelevant (does not add any new information to the question).

Name: ____________________

Date: ____________________

Basic Financial Math

OPEN RESPONSE #2

Please answer all parts of the question in the space provided.

Prompt: Danny and three friends went to the football game Friday night. It cost them $5 each to get into the game. While at the game, the four together had two orders of nachos ($2.50 each), four large colas ($1.50 each), four candy bars ($0.75 each), and two bags of popcorn ($1 each). At the end of the evening, they split the $20 gasoline bill to help Danny.

1. How much did each one spend Friday night? Show or explain how you got your answer.

2. How much would each have spent if only three of them split the gasoline bill? Show or explain how you got your answer.

Scoring Guide

4 Student gives correct answers for parts 1 and 2. All explanations are clear and complete. There is evidence of clear understanding of the concept.

3 Student gives correct answers for parts 1 and 2. Explanations are correct, but possibly unclear. There is less evidence of clear understanding.

2 Student answers 1 (1 or 2) part of the questions completely correct. There is some evidence of understanding.

1 Student gives only parts of correct answers. There is little evidence of understanding.

0 Response is totally incorrect or irrelevant (does not add any new information to the question).

The Financial Plan: Calculating Opportunity Cost and Income

You will need the following math concepts to begin planning for your financial future. You'll use the first concept—**calculating opportunity cost**—for decision-making purposes. Any time you select one option over another, you will have opportunity costs. Opportunity costs are specifically defined as the cost of the next best alternative. For example, if you decide to attend the football game on Friday night instead of working, you are incurring opportunity costs. You could have worked four hours and made $9 an hour. That's a total of $36 you could have made. In addition, you may have spent $10 at the game that you would not have spent at work. Therefore, in this example, your total cost for going to the game instead of working is $46. Your opportunity cost of going to the game was the $36 in foregone income. You will find most of the decisions you make involve some consideration of opportunity costs.

You will use the second concept—**calculating income**—for loan applications, tax purposes, and budgeting. You need to have an accurate assessment of income. This becomes particularly important for self-employed individuals. You can't count every dollar coming in as your personal income since you will also have expenses you must pay. Students may have income from working, scholarships, grants, and other sources.

The third concept—**forecasting income**—is very closely tied to calculating income except it is forward looking and used for planning purposes. Forecasting income enables you to make comprehensive budgets and determine areas where you might have excess funds. You need to be able to forecast your income over the coming months and years in order to budget savings and retirement properly.

Name: ____________________

Date: ____________________

The Financial Plan: Calculating Opportunity Cost and Income

CONCEPT #1: Calculating Opportunity Cost

Remember, opportunity costs are the cost of your next best alternative to some decision you make. For example, if you decide to attend technical school for one year instead of going straight to work, you may be forgoing making $9 an hour for 40 hours a week for 52 weeks a year. Your opportunity cost for attending school is therefore ($9 × 40) × 52 weeks = $18,720. This information is useful to you because you will want to determine how long it takes you to recover this investment in school.

Math Review

(8 × 4) + 10 = ________

(12 × 32) + 85 = ________

(56 × 6) + 453 = ________

(9 × 2) + 20 = ________

(11 × 50) + 115 = ________

(64 × 7) + 352 = ________

(7.50 × 8) + 100 = ________

(14 × 12) + 500 = ________

(72 × 6.50) + 920 = ________

(15 × 40) + 60 = ________

(10 × 25) + 160 = ________

(125 × 8) + 1,115 = ________

MyFinLitLab **Apply Your Knowledge**

1. Janice decided to go to the basketball game on Thursday night instead of working at the restaurant. What is her opportunity cost for this decision assuming she spent $24 in gas driving to the away game and $8 at the concession stand? Janice normally works 5 hours at the restaurant and makes $7 an hour plus tips. Her tips typically run about $35 on a weeknight.

2. Graham decided to play football this year instead of getting a part-time job. Last year he made about $1,100 during football season. He also spends about $9 on eating out after each game. His team plays a 10-game season. What is his opportunity cost of playing football?

3. Latron believes if he cuts back on his part-time job, he can spend some additional time working out over the next 20 weeks and earn an athletic scholarship to the local college. However, cutting back at work means he will forgo making $12 an hour at his uncle's shop. Assuming he now works only 10 hours a week with his reduced schedule instead of the normal 22 hours a week, how much will his scholarship have to pay for him to break even?

4. Amber would like to go on the field trip this Saturday. However, she was scheduled to work 10 hours and she makes $8.50 an hour. Additionally, the field trip activity fee was $30. What is her opportunity cost to go on the field trip?

5. Barinda is considering running for student government. However, she knows she will have to work about 10 hours fewer per week if elected, and she makes $7 an hour. The campaign will also cost her about $100 in campaign buttons and posters. What is her total cost for serving on student government if elected if she actively serves for 30 weeks?

Name: ______________________

Date: ______________________

CHAPTER 2

The Financial Plan: Calculating Opportunity Cost and Income

CONCEPT #2: Calculating Income

People generate income from several sources. We can get income from our jobs, allowances, or from financial investments. We need to know our income for several reasons, but the most common reason is for budgeting. We need to know how much money we have coming in so we can plan our outflows. For example, if you have a $750-a-month income, you need to make sure your outflow is less than $750 a month.

Math Review

(40 × 8) × 52 = ________

(789 × 52) + 2,000 = ________

(60 × 11.50) × 36 = ________

((60 × 14) × 52) + (25 × 52) = ________

(57 × 8.50) × 48 = ________

(500 × 52) + 1,100 = ________

(70 × 9.50) × 52 = ________

((40 × 18.50) × 52) + (35 × 52) = ________

(48 × 9) × 52 = ________

(625 × 52) + 965 = ________

(45 × 7.50) × 45 = ________

((55 × 12.25) × 52) + (50 × 52) = ________

(30 × 8.15) × 36 = ________

(125 × 52) + 1,565 = ________

(25 × 14.50) × 40 = ________

(15 × 9.25) × 52 + (125 × 40) = ________

MyFinLitLab

Apply Your Knowledge

1. Zeke earns about $500 a month at his job. He also gets a $100 a month allowance for doing his chores around the house. How much is his annual income?

2. Yolanda babysits for the couple next door. She averages making $50 a night and sits for three nights a month. She also works about 30 hours a month at the store and makes $8 an hour. What is her monthly income?

3. Brandon mows six yards once a week for 22 weeks. He averages making about $30 a yard but spends about $5 a yard on gasoline and mower maintenance. How much income does his yard business make him every year after considering expenses?

4. Tisha makes $6.50 an hour at the restaurant and about $10 an hour in tips. How much did she make last week when she worked 20 hours?

5. Gaylen works 40 hours every week during the summer and makes $11.50 an hour. In addition, he earns about $500 selling fireworks on the Fourth of July. How much did he make during a 12 week period in the summer?

Name: ______________________

Date: ______________________

The Financial Plan: Calculating Opportunity Cost and Income

CONCEPT #3: Forecasting Income

Forecasting income is important for budgeting purposes. When you construct next year's budget, you will need some estimate of income as the first step. For example, Luke makes $120 a week working part time at the grocery store. He also gets $25 a week for helping his dad around the house, and he mows his neighbor's yard for six weeks during the summer when his neighbor is on vacation. He gets $50 every time he mows the yard and he uses his neighbor's mower and gasoline. How much will Luke make next year? Luke expects to make (($120 + $25) × 52) + ($50 × 6) = $7,540 + $300 = $7,840 in total income next year.

Math Review

((8 × 9) × 12) + ((12 × 4) × 52) = _______

52 × 20 × 11.25 = _______

((10 × 20) × 52) + 3,000 = _______

(36 × 9.10) + (4 × 12 × 52) = _______

(11 × 10 × 20) + (12 × 8 × 32) = _______

(48 × 125) + 4,200 = _______

(26 × 8.50) + ((12 × 9) × 52) = _______

(52 × 150) + 6,500 = _______

MyFinLitLab Apply Your Knowledge

1. Musa expects to make about $400 next month working at his dad's booth. He will also get a $200 check for his birthday. What is his expected income next month?

2. Kevin was accepted to college and is making plans for next year's budget. He anticipates getting a part-time job and making about $80 a week. In addition, his federal grants will be about $3,000 per semester. What is his income expected to be during the 36-week school year?

3. Dina just accepted a new job. She expects to earn about $135 a week during the 34-week school year and $450 a week during the remainder of the year. How much should Dina earn next year?

4. Robert plans to take a second job during the summer. His current job pays $80 a week and he works all year. The second job will pay about $200 a week for the 15-week summer period. How much will Robert make next year?

5. Caina earned a scholarship of $6,000 next year. She also expects to receive a grant of $3,200 next year and will make another $400 per month working a part-time job. How much does she anticipate in income next year?

Name: ______________________

Date: ______________________

The Financial Plan: Calculating Opportunity Cost and Income

OPEN RESPONSE #1

Please answer all parts of the question in the space provided.

Prompt: Bryce wants to be a part of the golf team. This means he will have team practice three times a week. He will need to pay $10 a week in greens fees for 12 weeks. His work pays $8.50 per hour, and he now works 25 hours per week. If he joins the golf team he will have to cut back at work to 15 hours per week.

1. What is Bryce's opportunity cost for playing on the golf team? Show or explain how you got your answer.

2. Explain what opportunity cost is. Why is this concept important to the decision-making process in one's financial future?

Scoring Guide

4 Student gives correct answers for parts 1 and 2. All explanations are clear and complete. There is evidence of clear understanding of the concept.

3 Student gives correct answers for parts 1 and 2. Explanations are correct, but possibly unclear. There is less evidence of clear understanding.

2 Student answers 1 (1 or 2) part of the questions completely correct. There is some evidence of understanding.

1 Student gives only parts of correct answers. There is little evidence of understanding.

0 Response is totally incorrect or irrelevant (does not add any new information to the question).

Name: ______________________

Date: ______________________

The Financial Plan: Calculating Opportunity Cost and Income

OPEN RESPONSE #2

Please answer all parts of the question in the space provided.

Prompt: Violet sings with her group at the teen club two Fridays a month. Each member is paid $50 a night for four hours of work. She also receives $20 a week babysitting after school one day a week during the school year (39 weeks). During the summer, her group plays two week nights every week (13 weeks). She also babysits three days a week all summer, making $50 a week.

1. Violet wants to forecast her income. Explain the purpose of forecasting income.
2. How much will Violet make next year? Show or explain how you got your answer.

Scoring Guide

4 Student gives correct answers for parts 1 and 2. All explanations are clear and complete. There is evidence of clear understanding of the concept.

3 Student gives correct answers for parts 1 and 2. Explanations are correct, but possibly unclear. There is less evidence of clear understanding.

2 Student answers 1 (1 or 2) part of the questions completely correct. There is some evidence of understanding.

1 Student gives only parts of correct answers. There is little evidence of understanding.

0 Response is totally incorrect or irrelevant (does not add any new information to the question).

CHAPTER 3

Financial Decision Making: Calculating Cash Flows

As you continue planning your financial future, you will find the following math concepts useful. The first concept—**calculating cash inflow**—is necessary for budgeting. The first step toward achieving any financial goal is to determine where you are right now. In order to do that you will need to put together a budget. The first step in budgeting is calculating cash inflows.

The second step in budgeting is our second concept—**calculating cash outflow**. Once you correctly identify your cash inflows and cash outflows, you will be able to determine whether you have a surplus or deficit. If you have a deficit, you will have to try to determine ways to increase your cash inflows or decrease cash outflows. It sounds complex but is really very simple. Conversely, if you have a surplus, you can save and invest that surplus.

You will use the third concept—**calculating savings needed**— for making major purchases and retirement. For the moment we will focus on major purchases. For example, you might be trying to save $4,000 for college tuition next year. Or, maybe you are trying to accumulate $1,500 over the next two years for a down payment on a car. In any case, if you plan accordingly, you can begin to increase cash inflows or reduce cash outflows to the point where you can save the necessary amount.

Name: ____________________

Date: ____________________

CHAPTER 3

Financial Decision Making: Calculating Cash Flows

CONCEPT #1: Calculating Cash Inflow

Cash inflows include any monies you have coming in from any source. For example, maybe you work 12 hours a week and make \$7.50 an hour. In addition, you may get a \$25 a week allowance from your grandfather. Both of these are cash inflows. In this case your weekly cash inflow is (12 hours × \$7.50) + \$25 = \$90 + \$25 = \$115 a week.

Once you have figured your weekly or monthly cash inflows, you might want to ask how much your cash inflows will be over the course of a year. So, 52 weeks × \$115 = \$5,980 a year in cash inflows.

Math Review

(15 × 8) + 50 = ________

20 × 9 × 52) + 800 = ________

(10 × 9) + 35 = ________

(12 × 7.25 × 52) + 1,000 = ______________

(12 × 8.50 × 36) + (16 × 350) = ________

(20 × 6.75 × 34) + (18 × 250) = ________

(8 × 11.50 × 32) + (20 × 225) = ________

(32 × 11.50 × 40) + (12 × 275) = ________

MyFinLitLab Apply Your Knowledge

1. Jeremiah works 25 hours a month at the local lumber yard and makes \$10 an hour. He also cleans up about 15 construction sites a year for his uncle and gets paid \$125 per job. How much are his annual cash inflows?

2. Lucinda makes \$50 every Friday night babysitting and she also sold \$276 worth of clothes on eBay last week. What where her cash inflows last week?

3. Zeb makes about \$120 a week working in his mom's restaurant. He also gets a \$30 allowance from his grandparents every week to help them with some chores. How much is his weekly cash inflow?

4. Nilam's paycheck from the local store was \$87.50 last week. He also got a \$50 birthday gift from his aunt and sold an old guitar for \$250. What were his cash inflows last week?

5. Marielle helps her mom clean houses on weekends and gets paid \$25 per house. She helped clean four houses on Saturday. She also got a rebate check in the mail for \$35 from a video game she bought. How much were her cash inflows this week?

Name: ______________________

Date: ______________________

Financial Decision Making: Calculating Cash Flows

CONCEPT #2: Calculating Cash Outflow

Cash outflows include any monies we have going out for any reason. Any payments we make or any monies we spend for any reason are cash outflows. For budgeting purposes we need to make sure our cash outflows are less than our cash inflows. Otherwise, we will have to borrow money or take money from savings to cover the shortfall.

Let's look at an example. Last month you may have made a $125 motorcycle payment. In addition, you spent about $35 on gasoline and another $50 on eating out. In this case, your total monthly cash outflows were $125 + $35 + $50 = $210.

Math Review

12 + 345 + 67 = ________

45 + 1,204 + 786 = ________

238 + 74 + 2,398 = ________

71 + 532 + 98 = ________

63 + 4,412 + 851 = ________

924 + 18 + 5,145 = ________

63 + 12.32 + (12 × 250) = ________

78 + 37.12 + (129.57 × 12) = ________

126 + 32.54 + (12 × 110) = ________

15 + 687.21 + (234.21 × 12) = ________

MyFinLitLab Apply Your Knowledge

1. Ivan spent $23.53 on eating out this week, $40 on gasoline, and $20 on a school function. How much were his total cash outflows?

2. Ramon bought two new tires for his truck that cost $274. He also changed the oil and filter, which cost him $24.32 for supplies. How much did he spend on vehicle maintenance this month?

3. Jauna paid $18 for school lunches this week and bought some jewelry for $42.14. She also bought a new shirt at the mall for $19.99 with the $40 she got for her birthday. How much were her total cash outflows?

4. Billy was looking at his spending records. Last month he made a $225 truck payment, spent $23.58 on some jeans, ate out three times for $6.23 each time, and used 20 gallons of gasoline for which he paid $3.76 a gallon. How much were his total cash outflows?

5. Brian's car payment is $178.45 and his car insurance last year was $645. He also spent an average of $75 a month on gasoline and repairs. How much were his total cash outflows for his car last year?

Identify

Identify the following as either a cash inflow (I) or a cash outflow (O) by placing the appropriate letter in the blank beside each.

_______	rent paid	_______	birthday gift received
_______	car payment	_______	birthday gift given
_______	allowance	_______	tips made at work
_______	paycheck	_______	money from mowing yard
_______	water bill	_______	video game purchase

CHAPTER 3

Financial Decision Making: Calculating Cash Flows

CONCEPT #3: Calculating Savings

Some of our financial goals require us to begin saving prior to accomplishing those goals. For example, you may want to buy a new game console that costs $350, but you don't have the money right now. However, if you know you can save $45 a month given your current income, you can figure how long it will take you to save up the money. Simply divide $350 by $45 and you get 7.7. It will take approximately eight months to save enough money to buy the new game console.

There are hundreds of other purchases or events we may need to save money for. School, down payments on houses and cars, vacations, weddings, and investments may all require saving money.

Math Review

$450 ÷ 8 = _______

$1,000 ÷ ($12 × 40) = _______

$2,300 ÷ (40 × $9) = _______

$825 ÷ 12 = _______

$4,000 ÷ ($9.50 × 20) = _______

$1,400 ÷ (18 × $7.25) = _______

$1,600 ÷ (340 – 211) = _______

$3,400 ÷ (409 – 211) = _______

($5,500 × .20) ÷ (650 – 350) = _______

($11,000 × .10) ÷ (725 – 550) = _______

MyFinLitLab **Apply Your Knowledge**

1. How much will Jennifer need to save every month for the next six months in order to accumulate $500 for her vacation?

2. Marcos needs to save $2,000 for college next year. If he has 12 months before he needs the money, how much will he need to save every month?

3. How long will it take Bonita to save $1,000 for a down payment on a car if she makes $40 a night babysitting and she typically babysits every Friday and Saturday?

4. Rob wants to buy a new canoe that will cost $720. How long will it take him to save enough money to buy it if his cash inflows average about $420 a month and his current cash outflows are $360 a month?

5. How long will it take Harlan to save enough money to put a down payment on a motorcycle if the bike will cost $3,000 and he needs a 20 percent down payment and he can save about $75 a month?

Name: ______________________

Date: ______________________

Financial Decision Making: Calculating Cash Flows

OPEN RESPONSE #1

Please answer all parts of the question in the space provided.

Prompt: Cristian works 15 hours a week at his uncle's auto shop. He makes $8.25 per hour. In addition, Cristian works for his mother at the hair salon cleaning on Saturday mornings for $30 a week.

Cristian works to pay for his car. The payments are $189.65 a month and he plans for $65.00 a month on gasoline. His car insurance is $575 a year.

1. How much was Cristian's total cash inflow for last year? Show or explain how you got your answer.

2. How much were his total cash outflows for his car last year? Show or explain how you got your answer.

Scoring Guide

4 Student gives correct answers for parts 1 and 2. All explanations are clear and complete. There is evidence of clear understanding of the concept.

3 Student gives correct answers for parts 1 and 2. Explanations are correct, but possibly unclear. There is less evidence of clear understanding.

2 Student answers 1 (1 or 2) part of the questions completely correct. There is some evidence of understanding.

1 Student gives only parts of correct answers. There is little evidence of understanding.

0 Response is totally incorrect or irrelevant (does not add any new information to the question).

Name: ______________________

Date: ______________________

Financial Decision Making: Calculating Cash Flows

OPEN RESPONSE #2

Please answer all parts of the question in the space provided.

Prompt: Jeremy earns $100 a week working during the summer months. He wants to save for the family vacation during the school holiday break. Jeremy wants to have $500 saved for his vacation.

1. How much will Jeremy need to save each month for the next three months in order to accumulate $500 for his vacation? Show or explain how you got your answer.

2. Explain why saving is necessary for some of your financial goals.

Scoring Guide

4 Student gives correct answers for parts 1 and 2. All explanations are clear and complete. There is evidence of clear understanding of the concept.

3 Student gives correct answers for parts 1 and 2. Explanations are correct, but possibly unclear. There is less evidence of clear understanding.

2 Student answers 1 (1 or 2) part of the questions completely correct. There is some evidence of understanding.

1 Student gives only parts of correct answers. There is little evidence of understanding.

0 Response is totally incorrect or irrelevant (does not add any new information to the question).

CHAPTER 4

Calculating Your Net Worth

You can use the following math concepts to begin planning for your financial future. You will need the first concept—**calculating assets**—to determine your net worth. (You will see why net worth is important in a couple of paragraphs.) Assets are anything that you own, such as cars, clothing, houses, boats, stocks, mutual funds and so on. We classify assets in a number of different ways. For example, you may own stock, which is a financial asset. Your home would be a tangible or real asset. We also classify assets as liquid assets if you can convert them easily to cash within a short period of time without losing value. Liquid assets include cash, money in checking accounts, and money in savings accounts. Other less liquid assets such as stocks and bonds can be converted to cash quickly, but you may have to sell them at a discount.

The second concept—**calculating liabilities**—is the other component needed to calculate your net worth. Liabilities are anything that you owe. For example you may have an automobile loan at the bank on which you still owe $3,400 before it is paid in full. This amount is a liability. We also classify liabilities as current liabilities or long-term liabilities. Current liabilities are those that you will have to pay off within a year. Long-term liabilities, such as your home mortgage, may take 30 years to pay off.

You will also use the third concept—**calculating net worth**—many times throughout your lifetime. Net worth is specifically defined as your assets (things you own) minus your liabilities (debts you owe). The difference between your assets and liabilities is your net worth. Net worth is important because many lenders use this value to determine your creditworthiness. The higher your net worth, the more likely they are to loan you money. This is because you have assets you can sell in order to repay them if for some reason you have cash flow problems.

Name: ____________________

Date: ____________________

CHAPTER 4

Calculating Your Net Worth

CONCEPT #1: Calculating Assets

Remember, assets are anything that you own. Some of the things you own have significant value while others do not. For purposes of calculating your net worth, we typically exclude assets such as clothing, since in most cases you could get little or no money for your clothes if you needed to sell them.

Calculating assets usually is a relatively simple math problem. Let's assume Tabitha wants to know the total value of all of her assets. She has a car valued at $4,500, a computer worth $700, and jewelry valued at $450. What is the value of her assets? $4,500 + $700 + $450 = $5,650.

Math Review

69 + 743 = _______

259 + 3,100 + 870 = _______

5,815 + 650 = _______

51 + 239 = _______

718 + 2,122 + 315 = _______

9,125 + 860 = _______

87 + 321 = _______

198 + 8,230 + 4,500 = _______

11,520 + 450 = _______

55 + 622 = _______

820 + 7,300 + 5,050 = _______

100,000 + 7,500 = _______

(100 × 45.50) + (60 × 12.38) = _______

(80 × 32.25) + (200 × 35.88) = _______

MyFinLitLab **Apply Your Knowledge**

1. Granger has a boat worth $4,000 and a car worth about $8,000. He also has roughly $500 worth of tools. What is the value of his assets?

2. Samantha just bought a car for $4,500. She paid $500 down and took out a loan for the remainder. She also has $1,200 in a savings account. What is the value of her assets?

3. Malin has some jewelry she inherited from her grandmother worth about $3,200 and a motorcycle valued at $2,000. What is the value of her assets?

4. Latoya has 50 shares of stock in ABC company worth $35.75 a share, a car worth about $5,600, and a collection of figurines worth around $2,000. What is the value of her assets?

5. Cierra has 50 shares of stock in two different companies (100 total shares) worth $78.12 and $111.15 respectively. What is the value of these financial assets?

Name: ______________________

Date: ______________________

CHAPTER 4

Calculating Your Net Worth

CONCEPT #2: Calculating Liabilities

Remember, liabilities are any money that you owe either an individual or company. Common liabilities are the remaining money you owe for house payments (mortgages), car notes, phone leases, etc. Any amount we are obligated to repay is a liability. The difference between our assets and liabilities is our net worth, which we calculate in Concept #3.

Math Review

95 + 333 = ________

569 + 7,800 + 705 = ________

4,585 + 506 = ________

116 + 395 = ________

940 + 1,200 + 6,880 = ________

14,550 + 920 = ________

25 + 650 = ________

365 + 5,445 + 5,090 = ________

17,345 + 987 = ________

88 + 832 = ________

950 + 8,010 + 7,145 = ________

155,421 + 12,450 = ________

MyFinLitLab Apply Your Knowledge

1. Justus owes $500 to his uncle for money he borrowed to go on vacation, $1,500 on his car, and $674 on his credit card. How much are his total liabilities?

2. Karen overspent this month on her credit cards and owes $457.23 on one card and $874.12 on another card. She also owes $1,200 for the remainder of her tuition at the local college. What are her total liabilities?

3. Ian's parents owe $59,000 on their house, $4,500 on their car, and $3,020 on a boat. How much are their total liabilities?

4. Clay just bought a car and financed $15,000. He also owes $345 on his credit card. How much are his total liabilities?

5. Ashton borrowed $500 from his parents and $350 from his aunt to attend the first semester of trade school and to cover a portion of his costs. He also owes $400 for some tools he bought for the program. How much are his total liabilities?

Name: ____________________

Date: ____________________

CHAPTER 4

Calculating Your Net Worth

CONCEPT #3: Calculating Net Worth

Remember, net worth is your assets minus your liabilities. Net worth is often needed for loan applications and also is used as a scorecard for your financial health. Let's look at a particular example. Jericho needs to calculate his net worth in order to fill out the student loan application. His car is worth about $4,500, but he still owes $1,200 to the bank. His other assets include a four-wheeler worth about $2,300 and $1,000 in his bank account. He had no other debts. Jericho needs to sum up his assets and subtract the liabilities, so his net worth is $4,500 + $2,300 + $1,000 – $1,200 = $6,600.

Identify Assets (A) and Liabilities (L):

_______	Car	_______	House
_______	Car note	_______	Phone lease
_______	Clothes	_______	House payment
_______	Boat loan	_______	Jewelry
_______	Baseball cards	_______	Money owed to a friend
_______	IBM stock		

Math Review

(452 + 457) – 78 = _______	(129 + 731) – 82 = _______
(23 + 567) – 34 = _______	(51 + 162) – 41 = _______
(4,789 + 132 + 54) – 532 = _______	(3,911 + 514 + 54) – 325 = _______
(1,211 + 69) – 54 = _______	(527 + 587) – 125 = _______
(11 + 112) – 29 = _______	(79 + 624) – 95 = _______
(7,819 + 225 + 61) – 221 = _______	(1,948 + 841 + 12) – 982 = _______

MyFinLitLab **Apply Your Knowledge**

1. Cheyenne owns a car worth $5,200 and a motorcycle worth $2,600. Her only debt is the $800 she still owes her father for the car. How much is her net worth?

2. Garth's home entertainment system is worth about $1,200. He also owns some sports equipment valued at $300 and has $950 in a savings account. Garth owes one more payment of $50 on his entertainment system. What is Garth's net worth?

3. Lizzy's assets include her car worth about $7,500 and some stock her grandmother left her worth about $12,000. She still owes $1,500 on her car and about $400 that she borrowed from her brother for spring break. What is Lizzy's net worth?

4. Hsu owns 30 shares of Wal-Mart stock worth $48 a share and 50 shares of another company's stock worth about $61 a share. What is his net worth assuming he has no debt?

5. Nika wants to borrow some money from the bank and needs to determine her net worth. She has a car worth $3,400 and has $400 in her checking account. If her only debt is $600 she still owes on her car, what is her net worth?

Name: ____________________

Date: ____________________

Calculating Your Net Worth

OPEN RESPONSE #1

Please answer all parts of the question in the space provided.

Prompt: Abby is applying for a loan to go to art school. The application asked for her total assets. In her bedroom, Abby has an entertainment unit ($700), an IPod ($200), her drawing work desk that she got to take with her to school ($450), and the bedroom set ($1,200) that her parents told her could go with her to school.

She knows that there also are stocks given to her by her grandparents each birthday that are now worth $9,000.

1. What is the total of Abby's assets? Show or explain how you got your answer.

2. Explain to Abby the difference in tangible (real) assets versus financial assets.

Scoring Guide

4 Student gives correct answers for parts 1 and 2. All explanations are clear and complete. There is evidence of clear understanding of the concept.

3 Student gives correct answers for parts 1 and 2. Explanations are correct, but possibly unclear. There is less evidence of clear understanding.

2 Student answers 1 (1 or 2) part of the questions completely correct. There is some evidence of understanding.

1 Student gives only parts of correct answers. There is little evidence of understanding.

0 Response is totally incorrect or irrelevant (does not add any new information to the question).

Name: ______________________

Date: ______________________

Calculating Your Net Worth

OPEN RESPONSE #2

Please answer all parts of the question in the space provided.

Prompt: Vince wants to be able to tell his lender his net worth. He has a car ($7,580), an entertainment unit ($1,500), stocks (total worth $750), and all the furniture in his small apartment (total worth $2,360). Vince is still paying on a loan for his mechanic training. He has $3,390 remaining on the loan. There is also the $890 remainder due on his car loan.

1. What is Vince's net worth? Show or explain how you got your answer.

2. Explain to Vince how to calculate his net worth.

Scoring Guide

4 Student gives correct answers for parts 1 and 2. All explanations are clear and complete. There is evidence of clear understanding of the concept.

3 Student gives correct answers for parts 1 and 2. Explanations are correct, but possibly unclear. There is less evidence of clear understanding.

2 Student answers 1 (1 or 2) part of the questions completely correct. There is some evidence of understanding.

1 Student gives only parts of correct answers. There is little evidence of understanding.

0 Response is totally incorrect or irrelevant (does not add any new information to the question).

Calculating a Budget and Educational Investment

You can use the following math concepts in planning for your financial future. The first concept—**creating a budget**—is a necessary process that will help you accomplish your goals. A budget will force you to think about expenditures and how they impact your overall financial plan. It also will allow you to identify areas where you can trim expenditures or increase cash inflows in order to find money for saving.

The second concept—**calculating educational investment**—is necessary to determine whether or not to spend time and money on training and/or education. Education is an investment in your future earnings potential that is not costless. Not only do you spend money on tuition, books, and other supplies, but you also forgo income. In other words, the opportunity cost of education is important to consider. Spending some time calculating the out-of-pocket costs for education, and the lost income from working while attending school, is a good exercise. You can easily compare these costs to the expected benefit and make better decisions.

Name: ____________

Date: ____________

Calculating a Budget and Educational Investment

CONCEPT #1: Calculating a Budget

A budget is a forecast of future cash inflows and outflows. As you recall, in Chapter 3 we spent some time calculating current cash flows. Knowing your current cash flows is the starting place for your budget. Your budget is an important tool that should serve as a guide for your spending and help you spend less money than you make. Budgets also help us make decisions about purchases. If the money is not available in the budget, we should not spend it.

Math Review

$50 + 600 + (4 \times 65) =$ ______	$125 + 75 + 267 + (4 \times 125) =$ ______
$250 + 136 + (4 \times 29) =$ ______	$225 + 98 + 354 + (4 \times 175) =$ ______
$95 + 257 + (4 \times 55) =$ ______	$325 + 52 + 211 + (4 \times 112) =$ ______
$125 + 236 + (4.5 \times 80) =$ ______	$415 + 85 + 254 + (4 \times 210) =$ ______

MyFinLitLab **Apply Your Knowledge**

1. Grady makes $25 a week taking care of some chores around the house. He also makes $250 a week for 12 weeks during the summer. How much is Grady's annual income?

2. Grady spends an average of $40 a week on gasoline and eating out. How much of his summer income does Grady need to use to supplement his income during the school year?

3. Grady would like to spend $500 on a guitar. Will he have enough money to do that and supplement his income if he saves $100 a week of his summer money?

4. What if the guitar costs $1,000 instead?

5. What changes could Grady make that would give him enough money to buy the $1,000 guitar and still have spending money for the school year?

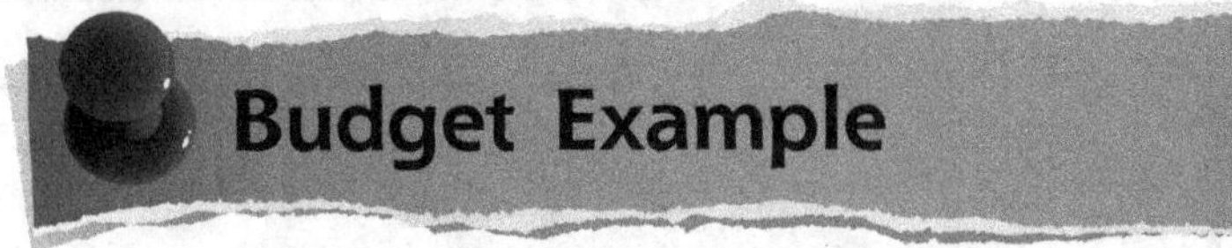

Budget Example

Jillian's take home (net) pay is about $2,300 a month. She also makes about $250 a month selling yard sale items on eBay. Her current rent is $500 a month and her car payment is $325 a month. She also spends about $45 a week on groceries. Jillian's electric bill averages about $85 a month and she pays $35 a month for cable television. Jillian allocates $100 a month for entertainment and clothing, $200 a month for gasoline and insurance on her car, and she puts $150 a month into a savings account for miscellaneous expenditures. She is trying to save money for a down payment on a home. Given her current situation, how much could she save annually toward her goal? To answer this question, you need to create an annual budget for Jillian.

Jillian's Annual Budget

Cash Inflows	**Monthly**	**Annual**
Salary	$2,300	$27,600
eBay income	250	3,000
Total Cash Inflows	2,550	30,600
Cash Outflows		
Rent	$500	$6,000
Car payment	325	3,900
Groceries*	195	2,340
Electric bill	85	1,020
Cable TV	35	420
Entertainment	100	1,200
Gas & insurance	200	2,400
Misc.	150	1,800
Total Cash Outflows	**$1,590**	**$19,080**
Net Cash Flows	$2,550 − $1,590 = +$960	+$11,520

**Note*: Since groceries cost $45 a week, you will need to multiply $45 × 52 weeks = $2,340 per year. Take $2,340 ÷ 12 months = $195 per month.

Jillian has a good bit of budget surplus. In fact, if she strictly adheres to her budget, she could save $11,520 toward her goal every year.

Name: ______________________

Date: ______________________

Budget Problem 1

Wayne averages bringing home $800 per month at his part-time job. However, he expects that next year he will make another $200 per month. His current expenses include a car payment of $250 a month. He pays another $100 a month for insurance and uses about $225 a month in gasoline. His repair bills on the car have averaged $100 a month for the past year. He also wants to help his mom out with groceries next year and expects to spend about $200 a month on this. Will he have any money remaining for entertainment?

Wayne's Annual Budget (next year's forecast)

Cash Inflows	**Monthly**	**Annual**
Salary		
Other income		
Total Cash Inflows		
Cash Outflows		
Rent		
Car payment		
Groceries		
Electric bill		
Cable TV		
Entertainment		
Gas & insurance		
Misc.		
Car repair bills		
Other		
Other		
Total Cash Outflows		
Net Cash Flows		

Name: ______________________

Date: ______________________

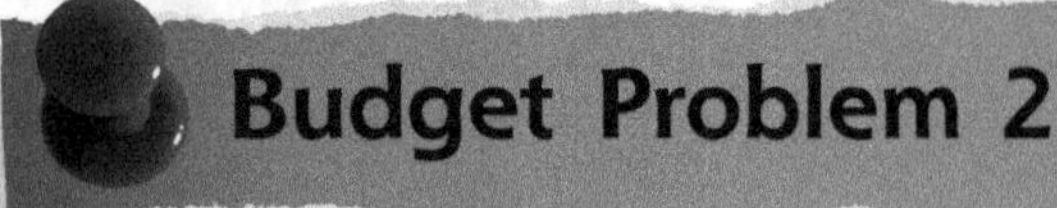

Budget Problem 2

Garth wants to save $3,000 to make an album. At his current job he usually brings home about $1,200 a month. However, he also intends to get a second job where he should make another $50 a week. His truck payment is $200 a month and he spends another $250 on gasoline and maintenance. Garth's truck insurance also costs him another $100 a month. He typically spends another $150 a month at the music store on supplies and music. After tracking his expenses for a month, he also knows he spends about $500 a month on eating out and entertainment. What will Garth need to do in order to achieve his goal?

Garth's Annual Budget

Cash Inflows	**Monthly**	**Annual**
Salary		
Other income		
Total Cash Inflows		
Cash Outflows		
Rent		
Car payment		
Groceries		
Electric bill		
Cable TV		
Entertainment		
Gas & insurance		
Misc.		
Total Cash Outflows		
Net Cash Flows		

Name: ______________________

Date: ______________________

CHAPTER 5

Calculating a Budget and Educational Investment

CONCEPT #2: Calculating for Educational Investment

Did you ever consider the fact that education is an investment in your future? However, not only do you invest the money you spend on education or training, but you also forgo income while pursuing a certification or degree. In this section, you will calculate the total cost of that education or training. After that, you can compare that cost with the difference in income you expect to receive after the training. Is it a good investment? At least now you know.

Math Review

(4 × 4,000) + 3,000 = _______

(2 × 5,200) + 1,800 = _______

(4 × 2,600) + 2,100 = _______

(4 × 1,950) + 18,000 = _______

(8 × 5,000) + (8 × 1,200) = _______

(8 × 3,700) + (8 × 900) = _______

(8 × 2,750) + (8 × 1,550) = _______

(8 × 4,250) + (8 × 875) = _______

MyFinLitLab **Apply Your Knowledge**

1. Jason found out that tuition for a two-year technical school will cost him about $3,500 per year. Books and supplies will cost another $1,100 per year. Assuming he will quit his job making $250 a week and devote all his time to the program, what will his total cost be for this training?

2. If Jason's training will allow him to get a job making $34,000 a year, how long will it take him to recover his initial investment?

3. Lindsey's college will cost her a total of $6,000 a year for the next four years. She is also forgoing making $26,000 a year at the local mall. However, she will be able to make about $8,000 a year while going to school. What is her total investment in education?

4. What would the difference in investment be if Lindsey did not work at all and was able to finish in three years?

5. Karam anticipates spending $8,400 a year for the next five years on his college education. He will also forgo making $12,000 a year during this time. How much will he invest in education?

Name: ______________________

Date: ______________________

Calculating a Budget and Educational Investment

OPEN RESPONSE #1

Please answer all parts of the question in the space provided.

Prompt: Beau is trying to set up a budget. He has come to you for information to set up the budget. Beau knows what his income is and what his expenses are, but does not know what to do next.

1. Explain to Beau how to set up a budget.
2. Once Beau has a budget, explain to him how he might be able to increase his savings.

Scoring Guide

4 Student gives correct answers for parts 1 and 2. All explanations are clear and complete. There is evidence of clear understanding of the concept.

3 Student gives correct answers for parts 1 and 2. Explanations are correct, but possibly unclear. There is less evidence of clear understanding.

2 Student answers 1 (1 or 2) part of the questions completely correct. There is some evidence of understanding.

1 Student gives only parts of correct answers. There is little evidence of understanding.

0 Response is totally incorrect or irrelevant (does not add any new information to the question).

Name: ______________________

Date: ______________________

CHAPTER 5

Calculating a Budget and Educational Investment

OPEN RESPONSE #2

Please answer all parts of the question in the space provided.

Prompt: Katherine's parents keep telling her that education is an investment. They want her to begin saving for her future. She plans to continue her education. Katherine has come to you to help her understand why education is an investment.

1. Explain to Katherine the possible costs of pursuing additional education.
2. Explain to Katherine how education can be an investment.

Scoring Guide

4 Student gives correct answers for parts 1 and 2. All explanations are clear and complete. There is evidence of clear understanding of the concept.

3 Student gives correct answers for parts 1 and 2. Explanations are correct, but possibly unclear. There is less evidence of clear understanding.

2 Student answers 1 (1 or 2) part of the questions completely correct. There is some evidence of understanding.

1 Student gives only parts of correct answers. There is little evidence of understanding.

0 Response is totally incorrect or irrelevant (does not add any new information to the question).

Taxes and Financial Planning

The following math concepts are used in financial planning. You can use the first concept—**calculating sales tax**—to determine where to purchase a big-ticket item such as furniture or consumer electronics. Since sales tax is often collected at the state and local level, it is not uncommon for a state to have numerous different sales taxes. A person might be able to drive just a few miles and save several dollars in tax on a major purchase.

The second concept—**calculating gross income**—relates to income tax. The first step in filing your annual income tax return is to determine how much money you made. Gross income is the total of all income you received from almost any source. You will see that some income, such as veteran's benefits, is excluded from gross income for tax purposes.

The third concept—**calculating your FICA withholdings**—is typically done by your employer. If you are on a payroll and taking part in the Social Security system, your employer withholds Social Security, or FICA taxes, from your paycheck. The employer then matches that amount and remits it to the federal government on your behalf. FICA is currently 4.2 percent of your income and is withheld on the first $110,100 of income as of 2011. If you make more than that, then you will not have a 4.2 percent FICA deduction on the earnings above $110,100. The amount of income subject to FICA tax is indexed to inflation and changes every year by increasing slightly. In addition to the 4.2 percent FICA withholdings, the government will collect 1.45 percent for Medicare. Medicare will be withheld from all your income and not capped like FICA. The typical FICA withholdings are 6.2 percent but this amount was reduced to 4.2 percent for the years 2011 and 2012 in an effort to stimulate economic growth.

The fourth concept—**calculating your tax liability using a simple income tax return**—is a process that you will have to do every year as long as you have an income. Your tax returns will likely become more and more complex as your earnings increase, but for now we will work with the U.S. Individual Income Tax Return Form 1040. Use the tax tables located at **http://www.irs.gov/pub/irs-pdf/i1040tt.pdf** to help you fill out this form.

Name: ____________________

Date: ____________________

Taxes and Financial Planning

CONCEPT #1: Calculating Sales Tax

As mentioned previously, sales tax calculations may be useful for determining where to purchase items. In fact, you may elect to make many major purchases over the Internet, since sales taxes on such purchases are not charged in most cases. As long as the cost of shipping does not exceed what you would pay in sales tax, you may be better off shopping online.

Let's look at one example. How much would Ryan pay in sales tax if he bought some furniture for $2,500 and the sales tax was 8.5 percent? The first step is to convert 8.5 percent to a decimal and then multiply by the item's price. So, 8.5 percent = .085. Therefore, the sales tax would be equal to $2,500 × .085 = $212.50. Ryan's total out-of-pocket costs for this purchase with sales tax are therefore $2,500 + $212.50 = $2,712.50. As you can see, sales taxes may make a big difference in the overall price you pay for an item.

Math Review

7.5% = ________

8 1/4% = ________

9.25% = ________

11 1/2% = ________

5.25% = ________

6 3/4% = ________

9.50% = ________

9 3/8% = ________

6% of 1,200 = ________

8.25% of $3,250 = ________

9 1/4% of 2,854 = ________

7 3/4% of 457.21 = ________

9 1/8% of 2,387.52 = ________

11 1/2% of 3,111 = ________

MyFinLitLab **Apply Your Knowledge**

1. How much sales tax will Justin pay on a computer priced at $1,723.42 if the sales tax rate is 9.25 percent?

2. Kari is thinking about buying an entertainment center that costs $750 on sale. If the sales tax rate is 7 1/2 percent how much money will she need in total to buy the entertainment center?

3. How much money will Gregg need to save in order to buy a video game for $75 if the sales tax is 8 1/8 percent?

4. Jauna is trying to decide where to buy her furniture. The living room set costs $1,200 in one nearby town and the sales tax is 9 percent. Another nearby town has the same living room set for $1,222 and the sales tax is 6¼ percent. Where should she shop?

5. How much sales tax will Liam pay on a $2,129 computer if the sales tax is 7⅜ percent?

Name: ____________________

Date: ____________________

Taxes and Financial Planning

CONCEPT #2: Calculating Gross Income

Gross income is a tax concept and therefore defined by the tax code. You will use gross income as an input on your tax return. Gross income is simply the income you receive from almost all sources. Income to be included in gross income includes wages and salary income, interest received, dividends, tips, rental income, scholarship amounts that exceed the cost of tuition and books, and others. The primary income exceptions that are not included in gross income are insurance reimbursements, child support payments received, veterans' benefits, welfare benefits, and moving expense reimbursements. A complete list of what to include or exclude from gross income is determined by the tax code and could change as new laws are passed. For practical reasons, verify your income sources by searching the IRS tax code. For the following problems, use the list of items just mentioned to determine whether to include them in gross income or exclude them from gross income.

Math Review

258 + 11,289 + 545 = ________

821 + 14,952 + 631 = ________

561 + 32,678 + 813 = ________

774 + 52,115 + 962 = ________

1,265 + 5,908 + 15,587 = ________

3,231 + 7,821 + 33,761 = ________

5,553 + 8,458 + 24,458 = ________

6,156 + 3,843 + 37,952 = ________

MyFinLitLab **Apply Your Knowledge**

1. Christen made $987 in tips last year, $5,891 in wages, and earned $786 in interest income. What was her gross income last year?

2. Corrie made $32,587 in salary last year, received $350 in interest income, and got a $1,000 bonus at work. How much was Corrie's gross income?

3. Malik's scholarship was $8,376 last year. His tuition and books cost $6,322. He also earned $7,398 at his job. What was Malik's gross income last year?

4. Vincent's new job as a state trooper paid him $42,119 in wages. He also worked a part-time job as a security guard and made another $5,400. What was Vincent's gross income last year?

5. Ramon's salary last year was $65,000. He also made another $23,000 in bonuses and commissions and earned another $2,300 in interest income. One stock he owns paid a dividend of $5 a share and he owns 400 shares. What was Ramon's gross income last year?

Name: ____________________

Date: ____________________

CHAPTER 6

Taxes and Financial Planning

CONCEPT #3: Calculating FICA Withholdings

FICA, more commonly known as Social Security, is withheld from many people's paychecks. In addition to the amount withheld, employers match employee contributions and remit that amount to the federal government. The FICA component includes 4.2 percent of your income and is withheld on the first $110,100 for 2011. This income level is indexed to inflation and therefore increases slightly every year. Another 1.45 percent is withheld from your check for Medicare. This amount is not income capped and will be withheld from every dollar of income. Keep in mind that the typical social security withholding is 6.2 percent but this amount was changed to 4.2 percent for the years 2011 and 2012.

Let's assume you made $45,600 in income during 2011. How much would be withheld from your check for Social Security? The answer is $45,600 × .042 = $1,915.20.

Math Review

$54,000 × .042 = ________	$78,000 × .0145 = ________
$32,980 × .124 = ________	$123,000 × .0145 = ________
$93,000 × .062 = ________	$112,300 × .0145 = ________
$75,332 × .124 = ________	$216,541 × .0145 = ________

MyFinLitLab **Apply Your Knowledge**

1. Maka made $45,670 last year. How much was withheld from her check for Social Security?

2. How much was withheld from Maka's check for Medicare?

3. Jocelyn's income for 2011 was $115,700. How much did she pay in Social Security tax?

4. How much did Jocelyn pay for Medicare tax?

5. What total amount was withheld from Jocelyn's check for Social Security and Medicare?

Name: ____________________

Date: ____________________

Taxes and Financial Planning

CONCEPT #4: Calculating Tax Liability

After you calculate your taxable income, you can determine your total tax liability by referring to the most recent tax tables. Remember, you begin by selecting the appropriate filing status and calculating your gross or total income and subtract out any allowable amounts, such as student loan interest paid, health savings account deductions, and others. You then subtract any standard deductions or itemized deductions to get to taxable income. At this point, you can calculate the tax that you owe for the year and compare it to the amount that has been paid via payroll withholdings. If you overpaid, you get a refund. If you underpaid, you will owe more taxes and have to send payment in with your tax return.

MyFinLitLab **Apply Your Knowledge**

Let's look at the following tax return for Jill N. Somebody and then use this format to complete another example with the information given.

Jill Somebody is single and made $34,550 last year in salary. She also had unemployment income of $1,000. Jill also paid $500 in student interest and had $3,891 withheld from her wages for federal taxes.

Now use the following information to fill out the blank Form 1040 on pages 62 and 63 and to compute Jimmy Anybody's tax liability:

Jimmy Anybody made $26,500 during 2011 and had $300 in interest income. He is single. His employer withheld $2,742 from his annual salary to pay federal taxes.

Form **1040** Department of the Treasury—Internal Revenue Service (99)
U.S. Individual Income Tax Return **2011** OMB No. 1545-0074 IRS Use Only—Do not write or staple in this space.

For the year Jan. 1–Dec. 31, 2011, or other tax year beginning , 2011, ending , 20 See separate instructions.

Your first name and initial	Last name	Your social security number
Jill N.	Somebody	111 11 1111
If a joint return, spouse's first name and initial	Last name	Spouse's social security number

Home address (number and street). If you have a P.O. box, see instructions. Apt. no.
1324 Anywhere St.

▲ Make sure the SSN(s) above and on line 6c are correct.

City, town or post office, state, and ZIP code. If you have a foreign address, also complete spaces below (see instructions).
Anytown, MD 11111

Foreign country name | Foreign province/county | Foreign postal code

Presidential Election Campaign
Check here if you, or your spouse if filing jointly, want $3 to go to this fund. Checking a box below will not change your tax or refund. ☐ You ☐ Spouse

Filing Status

Check only one box.

1 ☒ Single
2 ☐ Married filing jointly (even if only one had income)
3 ☐ Married filing separately. Enter spouse's SSN above and full name here. ▶
4 ☐ Head of household (with qualifying person). (See instructions.) If the qualifying person is a child but not your dependent, enter this child's name here. ▶
5 ☐ Qualifying widow(er) with dependent child

Exemptions

6a ☒ **Yourself.** If someone can claim you as a dependent, **do not** check box 6a
b ☐ **Spouse**

Boxes checked on 6a and 6b: 1

c **Dependents:**

(1) First name Last name	(2) Dependent's social security number	(3) Dependent's relationship to you	(4) ✓ if child under age 17 qualifying for child tax credit (see instructions)
			☐
			☐
			☐
			☐

If more than four dependents, see instructions and check here ▶☐

No. of children on 6c who:
• lived with you
• did not live with you due to divorce or separation (see instructions)
Dependents on 6c not entered above

d Total number of exemptions claimed — Add numbers on lines above ▶ 1

Income

Attach Form(s) W-2 here. Also attach Forms W-2G and 1099-R if tax was withheld.

If you did not get a W-2, see instructions.

Enclose, but do not attach, any payment. Also, please use **Form 1040-V.**

7	Wages, salaries, tips, etc. Attach Form(s) W-2			7	34,550 00
8a	**Taxable** interest. Attach Schedule B if required			8a	
b	**Tax-exempt** interest. **Do not** include on line 8a	8b			
9a	Ordinary dividends. Attach Schedule B if required			9a	
b	Qualified dividends	9b			
10	Taxable refunds, credits, or offsets of state and local income taxes			10	
11	Alimony received			11	
12	Business income or (loss). Attach Schedule C or C-EZ			12	
13	Capital gain or (loss). Attach Schedule D if required. If not required, check here ▶ ☐			13	
14	Other gains or (losses). Attach Form 4797			14	
15a	IRA distributions	15a	b Taxable amount	15b	
16a	Pensions and annuities	16a	b Taxable amount	16b	
17	Rental real estate, royalties, partnerships, S corporations, trusts, etc. Attach Schedule E			17	
18	Farm income or (loss). Attach Schedule F			18	
19	Unemployment compensation			19	1,000 00
20a	Social security benefits	20a	b Taxable amount	20b	
21	Other income. List type and amount			21	
22	Combine the amounts in the far right column for lines 7 through 21. This is your **total income** ▶			22	35,550 00

Adjusted Gross Income

Line	Description	Line	Amount	Line	Amount
23	Educator expenses	23			
24	Certain business expenses of reservists, performing artists, and fee-basis government officials. Attach Form 2106 or 2106-EZ	24			
25	Health savings account deduction. Attach Form 8889	25			
26	Moving expenses. Attach Form 3903	26			
27	Deductible part of self-employment tax. Attach Schedule SE	27			
28	Self-employed SEP, SIMPLE, and qualified plans	28			
29	Self-employed health insurance deduction	29			
30	Penalty on early withdrawal of savings	30			
31a	Alimony paid b Recipient's SSN ▶	31a			
32	IRA deduction	32			
33	Student loan interest deduction	33	500 00		
34	Tuition and fees. Attach Form 8917	34			
35	Domestic production activities deduction. Attach Form 8903	35			
36	Add lines 23 through 35			36	500 00
37	Subtract line 36 from line 22. This is your **adjusted gross income** ▶			37	35,050 00

For Disclosure, Privacy Act, and Paperwork Reduction Act Notice, see separate instructions. Cat. No. 11320B Form **1040** (2011)

Tax and Credits

Line	Description		Amount
38	Amount from line 37 (adjusted gross income)	38	35,050 00
39a	Check if: ☐ **You** were born before January 2, 1947, ☐ Blind. ☐ **Spouse** was born before January 2, 1947, ☐ Blind. **Total boxes checked ▶ 39a** ☐		
b	If your spouse itemizes on a separate return or you were a dual-status alien, check here ▶ 39b ☐		
40	**Itemized deductions** (from Schedule A) **or** your **standard deduction** (see left margin)	40	5,800 00
41	Subtract line 40 from line 38	41	29,250 00
42	**Exemptions.** Multiply $3,700 by the number on line 6d	42	3,700 00
43	**Taxable income.** Subtract line 42 from line 41. If line 42 is more than line 41, enter -0-	43	25,550 00
44	**Tax** (see instructions). Check if any from: **a** ☐ Form(s) 8814 **b** ☐ Form 4972 **c** ☐ 962 election	44	3,411 00
45	**Alternative minimum tax** (see instructions). Attach Form 6251	45	0
46	Add lines 44 and 45 ▶	46	3,411 00
47	Foreign tax credit. Attach Form 1116 if required	47	
48	Credit for child and dependent care expenses. Attach Form 2441	48	
49	Education credits from Form 8863, line 23	49	
50	Retirement savings contributions credit. Attach Form 8880	50	
51	Child tax credit (see instructions)	51	
52	Residential energy credits. Attach Form 5695	52	
53	Other credits from Form: **a** ☐ 3800 **b** ☐ 8801 **c** ☐	53	
54	Add lines 47 through 53. These are your **total credits**	54	0
55	Subtract line 54 from line 46. If line 54 is more than line 46, enter -0- ▶	55	3,411 00

Standard Deduction for—
- People who check any box on line 39a or 39b **or** who can be claimed as a dependent, see instructions.
- All others:

Single or Married filing separately, $5,800

Married filing jointly or Qualifying widow(er), $11,600

Head of household, $8,500

Other Taxes

Line	Description		Amount
56	Self-employment tax. Attach Schedule SE	56	
57	Unreported social security and Medicare tax from Form: **a** ☐ 4137 **b** ☐ 8919	57	
58	Additional tax on IRAs, other qualified retirement plans, etc. Attach Form 5329 if required	58	
59a	Household employment taxes from Schedule H	59a	
b	First-time homebuyer credit repayment. Attach Form 5405 if required	59b	
60	Other taxes. Enter code(s) from instructions	60	
61	Add lines 55 through 60. This is your **total tax** ▶	61	3,411 00

Payments

Line	Description		Amount
62	Federal income tax withheld from Forms W-2 and 1099	62	3,891 00
63	2011 estimated tax payments and amount applied from 2010 return	63	
64a	**Earned income credit (EIC)**	64a	
b	Nontaxable combat pay election 64b		
65	Additional child tax credit. Attach Form 8812	65	
66	American opportunity credit from Form 8863, line 14	66	
67	First-time homebuyer credit from Form 5405, line 10	67	
68	Amount paid with request for extension to file	68	
69	Excess social security and tier 1 RRTA tax withheld	69	
70	Credit for federal tax on fuels. Attach Form 4136	70	
71	Credits from Form: **a** ☐ 2439 **b** ☐ 8839 **c** ☐ 8801 **d** ☐ 8885	71	
72	Add lines 62, 63, 64a, and 65 through 71. These are your **total payments** ▶	72	3,891 00

If you have a qualifying child, attach Schedule EIC.

Refund

Line	Description		Amount
73	If line 72 is more than line 61, subtract line 61 from line 72. This is the amount you **overpaid**	73	480 00
74a	Amount of line 73 you want **refunded to you.** If Form 8888 is attached, check here ▶ ☐	74a	480 00
▶ b	Routing number ▶ **c** Type: ☐ Checking ☐ Savings		
▶ d	Account number		
75	Amount of line 73 you want **applied to your 2012 estimated tax** ▶	75	

Direct deposit? See instructions.

Amount You Owe

Line	Description		Amount
76	**Amount you owe.** Subtract line 72 from line 61. For details on how to pay, see instructions ▶	76	
77	Estimated tax penalty (see instructions)	77	

Third Party Designee

Do you want to allow another person to discuss this return with the IRS (see instructions)? ☐ **Yes.** Complete below. ☒ **No**

Designee's name ▶ Phone no. ▶ Personal identification number (PIN) ▶

Sign Here

Under penalties of perjury, I declare that I have examined this return and accompanying schedules and statements, and to the best of my knowledge and belief, they are true, correct, and complete. Declaration of preparer (other than taxpayer) is based on all information of which preparer has any knowledge.

Joint return? See instructions. Keep a copy for your records.

Your signature	Date	Your occupation	Daytime phone number
Jill Somebody	3/10/12	Teacher	111 111-1111
Spouse's signature. If a joint return, **both** must sign.	Date	Spouse's occupation	If the IRS sent you an Identity Protection PIN, enter it here (see inst.)

Paid Preparer Use Only

Print/Type preparer's name	Preparer's signature	Date	Check ☐ if self-employed	PTIN
Firm's name ▶		Firm's EIN ▶		
Firm's address ▶		Phone no.		

Form **1040** (2011)

Form **1040** Department of the Treasury—Internal Revenue Service (99)

U.S. Individual Income Tax Return 2011

OMB No. 1545-0074 | IRS Use Only—Do not write or staple in this space.

For the year Jan. 1–Dec. 31, 2011, or other tax year beginning , 2011, ending , 20 | See separate instructions.

Your first name and initial	Last name	Your social security number
If a joint return, spouse's first name and initial	Last name	Spouse's social security number
Home address (number and street). If you have a P.O. box, see instructions.	Apt. no.	▲ Make sure the SSN(s) above and on line 6c are correct.
City, town or post office, state, and ZIP code. If you have a foreign address, also complete spaces below (see instructions).		**Presidential Election Campaign** Check here if you, or your spouse if filing jointly, want $3 to go to this fund. Checking a box below will not change your tax or refund. ☐ You ☐ Spouse
Foreign country name	Foreign province/county	Foreign postal code

Filing Status

Check only one box.

1 ☐ Single
2 ☐ Married filing jointly (even if only one had income)
3 ☐ Married filing separately. Enter spouse's SSN above and full name here. ▶
4 ☐ Head of household (with qualifying person). (See instructions.) If the qualifying person is a child but not your dependent, enter this child's name here. ▶
5 ☐ Qualifying widow(er) with dependent child

Exemptions

6a ☐ **Yourself.** If someone can claim you as a dependent, **do not** check box 6a
b ☐ **Spouse**

} **Boxes checked on 6a and 6b**

c **Dependents:**

(1) First name Last name	(2) Dependent's social security number	(3) Dependent's relationship to you	(4) ✓ if child under age 17 qualifying for child tax credit (see instructions)
			☐
			☐
			☐
			☐

If more than four dependents, see instructions and check here ▶ ☐

No. of children on 6c who:
• lived with you
• did not live with you due to divorce or separation (see instructions)
Dependents on 6c not entered above

d Total number of exemptions claimed

Add numbers on lines above ▶

Income

Attach Form(s) W-2 here. Also attach Forms W-2G and 1099-R if tax was withheld.

If you did not get a W-2, see instructions.

Enclose, but do not attach, any payment. Also, please use **Form 1040-V.**

7	Wages, salaries, tips, etc. Attach Form(s) W-2		7
8a	**Taxable** interest. Attach Schedule B if required		8a
b	**Tax-exempt** interest. **Do not** include on line 8a	8b	
9a	Ordinary dividends. Attach Schedule B if required		9a
b	Qualified dividends	9b	
10	Taxable refunds, credits, or offsets of state and local income taxes		10
11	Alimony received		11
12	Business income or (loss). Attach Schedule C or C-EZ		12
13	Capital gain or (loss). Attach Schedule D if required. If not required, check here ▶ ☐		13
14	Other gains or (losses). Attach Form 4797		14
15a	IRA distributions 15a	b Taxable amount	15b
16a	Pensions and annuities 16a	b Taxable amount	16b
17	Rental real estate, royalties, partnerships, S corporations, trusts, etc. Attach Schedule E		17
18	Farm income or (loss). Attach Schedule F		18
19	Unemployment compensation		19
20a	Social security benefits 20a	b Taxable amount	20b
21	Other income. List type and amount		21
22	Combine the amounts in the far right column for lines 7 through 21. This is your **total income** ▶		22

Adjusted Gross Income

23	Educator expenses	23	
24	Certain business expenses of reservists, performing artists, and fee-basis government officials. Attach Form 2106 or 2106-EZ	24	
25	Health savings account deduction. Attach Form 8889	25	
26	Moving expenses. Attach Form 3903	26	
27	Deductible part of self-employment tax. Attach Schedule SE	27	
28	Self-employed SEP, SIMPLE, and qualified plans	28	
29	Self-employed health insurance deduction	29	
30	Penalty on early withdrawal of savings	30	
31a	Alimony paid b Recipient's SSN ▶	31a	
32	IRA deduction	32	
33	Student loan interest deduction	33	
34	Tuition and fees. Attach Form 8917	34	
35	Domestic production activities deduction. Attach Form 8903	35	
36	Add lines 23 through 35		36
37	Subtract line 36 from line 22. This is your **adjusted gross income** ▶		37

For Disclosure, Privacy Act, and Paperwork Reduction Act Notice, see separate instructions. Cat. No. 11320B Form **1040** (2011)

Tax and Credits

38	Amount from line 37 (adjusted gross income)		38
39a	Check if: { ☐ **You** were born before January 2, 1947, ☐ Blind. / ☐ **Spouse** was born before January 2, 1947, ☐ Blind. } **Total boxes checked** ▶ 39a ☐		
b	If your spouse itemizes on a separate return or you were a dual-status alien, check here ▶ 39b ☐		
40	**Itemized deductions** (from Schedule A) **or** your **standard deduction** (see left margin)		40
41	Subtract line 40 from line 38		41
42	**Exemptions.** Multiply $3,700 by the number on line 6d		42
43	**Taxable income.** Subtract line 42 from line 41. If line 42 is more than line 41, enter -0-		43
44	**Tax** (see instructions). Check if any from: **a** ☐ Form(s) 8814 **b** ☐ Form 4972 **c** ☐ 962 election		44
45	**Alternative minimum tax** (see instructions). Attach Form 6251		45
46	Add lines 44 and 45 ▶		46
47	Foreign tax credit. Attach Form 1116 if required	47	
48	Credit for child and dependent care expenses. Attach Form 2441	48	
49	Education credits from Form 8863, line 23	49	
50	Retirement savings contributions credit. Attach Form 8880	50	
51	Child tax credit (see instructions)	51	
52	Residential energy credits. Attach Form 5695	52	
53	Other credits from Form: **a** ☐ 3800 **b** ☐ 8801 **c** ☐ ______	53	
54	Add lines 47 through 53. These are your **total credits**		54
55	Subtract line 54 from line 46. If line 54 is more than line 46, enter -0- ▶		55

Standard Deduction for—
- People who check any box on line 39a or 39b **or** who can be claimed as a dependent, see instructions.
- All others:

Single or Married filing separately, $5,800

Married filing jointly or Qualifying widow(er), $11,600

Head of household, $8,500

Other Taxes

56	Self-employment tax. Attach Schedule SE	56
57	Unreported social security and Medicare tax from Form: **a** ☐ 4137 **b** ☐ 8919	57
58	Additional tax on IRAs, other qualified retirement plans, etc. Attach Form 5329 if required	58
59a	Household employment taxes from Schedule H	59a
b	First-time homebuyer credit repayment. Attach Form 5405 if required	59b
60	Other taxes. Enter code(s) from instructions ______	60
61	Add lines 55 through 60. This is your **total tax** ▶	61

Payments

62	Federal income tax withheld from Forms W-2 and 1099	62	
63	2011 estimated tax payments and amount applied from 2010 return	63	
64a	**Earned income credit (EIC)**	64a	
b	Nontaxable combat pay election 64b		
65	Additional child tax credit. Attach Form 8812	65	
66	American opportunity credit from Form 8863, line 14	66	
67	First-time homebuyer credit from Form 5405, line 10	67	
68	Amount paid with request for extension to file	68	
69	Excess social security and tier 1 RRTA tax withheld	69	
70	Credit for federal tax on fuels. Attach Form 4136	70	
71	Credits from Form: **a** ☐ 2439 **b** ☐ 8839 **c** ☐ 8801 **d** ☐ 8885	71	
72	Add lines 62, 63, 64a, and 65 through 71. These are your **total payments** ▶		72

If you have a qualifying child, attach Schedule EIC.

Refund

73	If line 72 is more than line 61, subtract line 61 from line 72. This is the amount you **overpaid**		73
74a	Amount of line 73 you want **refunded to you.** If Form 8888 is attached, check here ▶ ☐		74a
▶ b	Routing number ▶ **c** Type: ☐ Checking ☐ Savings		
▶ d	Account number		
75	Amount of line 73 you want **applied to your 2012 estimated tax** ▶	75	

Direct deposit? See instructions.

Amount You Owe

76	**Amount you owe.** Subtract line 72 from line 61. For details on how to pay, see instructions ▶		76
77	Estimated tax penalty (see instructions)	77	

Third Party Designee

Do you want to allow another person to discuss this return with the IRS (see instructions)? ☐ **Yes.** Complete below. ☐ **No**

Designee's name ▶ Phone no. ▶ Personal identification number (PIN) ▶

Sign Here

Under penalties of perjury, I declare that I have examined this return and accompanying schedules and statements, and to the best of my knowledge and belief, they are true, correct, and complete. Declaration of preparer (other than taxpayer) is based on all information of which preparer has any knowledge.

Joint return? See instructions. Keep a copy for your records.

Your signature	Date	Your occupation	Daytime phone number
Spouse's signature. If a joint return, **both** must sign.	Date	Spouse's occupation	If the IRS sent you an Identity Protection PIN, enter it here (see inst.)

Paid Preparer Use Only

Print/Type preparer's name	Preparer's signature	Date	Check ☐ if self-employed	PTIN
Firm's name ▶		Firm's EIN ▶		
Firm's address ▶		Phone no.		

Name: ______________________

Date: ______________________

CHAPTER 6

Taxes and Financial Planning

OPEN RESPONSE #1

Please answer all parts of the question in the space provided.

Prompt: Lizbeth is looking at her paycheck. She sees that she worked 29 hours this last week. She knows that she makes $6.75 an hour at her new job. What she does not understand is how they calculated FICA taxes. That really took a chunk out of her pay.

1. Calculate Lizbeth's gross income. Show or explain how you got your answer.

2. Explain to Lizbeth FICA withholdings.

3. If 4.2% is collected for Social Security and 1.45% is collected for Medicare from Lizbeth's paycheck, calculate her net income (gross income minus withholdings). Show or explain how you got your answer. Ignore federal and state taxes for this problem.

Scoring Guide

4 Student gives correct answers for parts 1–3. All explanations are clear and complete. There is evidence of clear understanding of the concept.

3 Student gives correct answers for parts 1–3. Explanations are correct, but possibly unclear. There is less evidence of clear understanding.

2 Student fails to answer at least one of the parts correctly. There is some evidence of understanding.

1 Student gives only parts of correct answers. There is little evidence of understanding.

0 Response is totally incorrect or irrelevant (does not add any new information to the question).

Name: ____________________

Date: ____________________

Taxes and Financial Planning

OPEN RESPONSE #2

Please answer all parts of the question in the space provided.

Prompt: Giuseppe is filing his first tax return. He earned $12,670 last year in salary. He will file as a single person. Giuseppe has a 1040 to file his tax return.

1. Explain to Giuseppe the steps he needs to follow to fill out his 1040.
2. Explain to Giuseppe the difference in getting a tax refund or paying more taxes. How will he know which he has to do?

Scoring Guide

4 Student gives correct answers for parts 1 and 2. All explanations are clear and complete. There is evidence of clear understanding of the concept.

3 Student gives correct answers for parts 1 and 2. Explanations are correct, but possibly unclear. There is less evidence of clear understanding.

2 Student answers 1 (1 or 2) part of the questions completely correct. There is some evidence of understanding.

1 Student gives only parts of correct answers. There is little evidence of understanding.

0 Response is totally incorrect or irrelevant (does not add any new information to the question).

Insurance: Life & Health

You will need the following math concepts in planning for your financial future. Insurance is a risk-reduction tool used to limit your financial exposure in the event you have some type of covered loss. When you purchase any type of insurance, you are protecting your assets from loss by buying the promise of a cash inflow that will begin with the occurrence of some event. If you buy insurance on your house, the event may be a fire or tornado that destroys the house. Your insurance will then reimburse you for the loss. In the case of health insurance, the event will be some covered illness or accident. In the case of life insurance, the event will be the death of the insured. In any case, the purchase of insurance protects you from having to pay the entire expense associated with the event that triggers the coverage. The following concepts are some things you will consider when shopping for insurance.

The first concept—**calculating out-of-pocket costs**—is important to understand when you actually use your health insurance coverage. Health insurance policies have two features that factor into this calculation: deductibles and co-insurance, or co-pay. Most policies have a deductible of some specified amount, such as $500 or $1,000. This amount is the portion of your medical claims that you will pay before the policy begins sharing the cost with you. For example, if you have a covered medical event that costs $3,000 and you have a $500 deductible, then you will pay the first $500. At that point, the insurance company will begin paying its share of the remaining $2,500. The share that the insurance company pays will be determined by your co-pay. Co-pays, or co-insurance, are most often expressed as a percentage of the covered amount. A co-pay of 20 percent is very common. In the case of a 20 percent co-pay, the insurance company will pay 80 percent of the amount remaining after the deductible is applied.

The second concept—**determining how much life insurance coverage you need**—is critical to protecting your loved ones in the event of your death. Life insurance proceeds help pay bills, educate dependents, and provide some security for those you leave behind. But, how much is enough? We'll look at a couple of methods to determine how much coverage you might need.

The third concept—**comparing insurance costs (health)**—is essential to budgeting. You need to be able to allocate a portion of your income for health insurance, and all policies are a little different in what they cover and what they cost. In most cases, the best option will be to secure health-insurance coverage through your employer. However, this coverage will not always be available. There is no fixed rule in determining which option is better for you. Be sure to research and do comparisons of all your options before making a decision.

Name: ______________________

Date: ______________________

Insurance: Life & Health

CONCEPT #1: Calculating Out-of-Pocket Costs

Let's look at the opening scenario. Assume you have a covered medical event that cost $3,000 and you have an insurance policy that has a $500 deductible and a 20 percent co-pay. In this instance you would pay $500 + .20($3,000 – $500) = $1,000.

Math Review

500 + .20(12,000 – 500) = _______

1,000 + .20(4,000 – 1,000) = _______

500 + .30(9,000 – 500) = _______

1,000 + .30(6,000 – 1,000) = _______

2,000 + .20(24,000 – 2,000) = _______

2.000 + .30(51,000 – 2,000) = _______

5,000 + .20(25,000 – 5,000) = _______

5,000 + .30(30,000 – 5,000) = _______

MyFinLitLab **Apply Your Knowledge**

1. Jennifer's insurance had a $500 deductible and a 20 percent co-pay. She had a covered medical event that cost $4,500. How much did she have to pay?

2. Kareem's insurance coverage through his work had a $500 deductible and a 30 percent co-pay. His skiing accident cost $7,200 in medical bills and was a covered event. How much are his out-of-pocket costs?

3. Larue broke his leg and incurred medical costs of $4,200. Assuming he has a $1,000 deductible and a 20 percent co-pay, how much will he have to pay for the accident?

4. Bianca injured her wrist and had to go to the emergency room at the local hospital. The total bill was $1,850. Assuming she has a $500 deductible and 30 percent co-pay, how much will she have to pay out-of-pocket?

5. How much will the insurance company pay on Mica's $17,000 hospital bill if she has a $5,000 deductible and 20 percent co-pay?

Name: ______________________

Date: ______________________

Insurance: Life & Health

CONCEPT #2: Determining How Much Life Insurance Coverage You Need

Individuals purchase life insurance to protect their loved ones from financial hardship in the event of their death. For example, a husband might purchase life insurance listing his wife as the beneficiary. If the policy is a $100,000 policy the wife will receive $100,000 in the event the husband dies. The $100,000 is the death benefit of this particular policy. Individuals can buy virtually any amount of life insurance coverage and typically pay monthly premiums to purchase life insurance. This exercise helps you determine how much life insurance to buy—that is, how large a death benefit you'd like your survivors to receive—given your circumstances. It does not discuss the cost of that insurance.

The income method of determining how much life insurance you need is a simple rule of thumb. You calculate your annual income and multiply by some multiple. A common multiple used is 10, although older couples may elect a lower multiple, since a lot of their needs may be met with accumulated savings. That is, they expect that they will have money in the bank that will help any survivor meet future expenses. Others with more children and/or little savings may elect to use higher multiples to prepare for higher college costs or other future expenses. There is no specific technique used to determine the exact multiple you will need to use. But remember that the more cash you expect your beneficiaries to need at your death, the higher the multiple you will need to use.

Let's look at an example. Janelle and Bob have two young children and limited savings. Their combined income is $84,000 and their insurance agent recommended using a multiple of ten times their income to calculate how much life insurance they need. In this example they need $84,000 × 10 = $840,000 worth of life insurance coverage.

Math Review

5 × 45,000 = _______

10 × 102,000 = _______

20 × 75,000 = _______

20 × 51,500 = _______

10 × (33,000 + 48,000) = _______

10 × (89,000 + 34,000) = _______

20 × (21,000 + 79,500) = _______

5 × (125,000 + 35,000) = _______

MyFinLitLab **Apply Your Knowledge**

1. Jermaine and Tabitha are in their late 50s and have significant savings. They believe a multiple of five times their income for life insurance is sufficient. Jermaine makes about $78,000 a year and Tabitha makes $115,000 per year. How much life insurance should they purchase?

2. Gayle makes about $45,000 a year and has one dependent daughter. Her savings are minimal, so she believes she needs a life insurance multiple of 20. How much life insurance should she buy?

3. Misty and Jake have a combined income of $77,000 a year. They have no children but limited savings. Their insurance agent told them a multiple of 10 would work for them. How much life insurance will they need to purchase?

4. Demetrius is single but would like to take care of his mother in the event of his death. He would like to replace her income of $25,000 a year with a multiple of 30. How much life insurance should he buy?

5. Sherry just purchased 20 times her annual income in life insurance. She has one job where she makes about $55,000 a year and she does some freelance work and makes another $24,000 a year. How much insurance did she purchase?

Name: ______________________

Date: ______________________

CHAPTER 7

Insurance: Life & Health

CONCEPT #3: Comparing Insurance Costs (Health)

Healthcare plans are usually classified as indemnity plans or managed care plans. Indemnity plans allow participants to seek health care from any qualified medical provider. Managed health-care plans limit your choice of health-care provider to a specific list of physicians and other medical professionals. Getting care from someone outside of this network may not be covered or may require higher co-pays. Regardless of the option available, you should be aware of the following issues.

The two most common types of provider networks are Health Maintenance Organizations (HMOs) and Preferred Provider Organizations (PPOs). HMOs are based on negotiated agreements with specific doctors to provide health care. Individuals select a primary care physician from an approved list and must get referrals for any additional specialized care. That primary care doctor may approve and arrange for care from a specialist—and set limits on the number of times the patient may visit. PPOs function in a similar fashion, but they generally provide a larger network of providers. In return for this greater flexibility, PPOs typically cost more than HMOs.

All plans differ in cost or premium that you pay. Sometimes your employer will share in this cost and therefore reduce the amount you have to pay out-of-pocket. In many instances you may have to pay 100 percent of the premium. In addition to the premium you pay, there is co-insurance, or co-pay, that differs from plan to plan. Health insurance plans also have various levels of deductibles.

You will also note that many health insurance plans do not cover vision and dental expense unless you add those items and pay higher premiums. Pay close attention to the types of coverage your plan will actually pay for. All of these differences make shopping for health insurance difficult. Rarely is one plan always the best for every individual.

Activity #1

Using the chart below, research the features and costs of three different types of health insurance plans. You can ask your parents, a family friend, an employer, or go on the Internet for your research.

	Indemnity Plan	HMO	PPO
Health Insurance Options			
Premium Co-Pay If Yes, Amount	☐ Yes ☐ No $	☐ Yes ☐ No $	☐ Yes ☐ No $
Coverage Eligibility	☐ Self ☐ Family	☐ Self ☐ Family	☐ Self ☐ Family
Coverage			
In State	☐ Yes ☐ No	☐ Yes ☐ No	☐ Yes ☐ No
Out of State	☐ Yes ☐ No	☐ Yes ☐ No	☐ Yes ☐ No

Out of Country	☐ Yes ☐ No	☐ Yes ☐ No	☐ Yes ☐ No
Prescription Coverage If Yes, Amount of Co-Pay	☐ Yes ☐ No $	☐ Yes ☐ No $	☐ Yes ☐ No $
Office Visits			
Co-Pay Amount	$	$	$
Annual Deductible If Yes, Amount of Deductible	☐ Yes ☐ No $	☐ Yes ☐ No $	☐ Yes ☐ No $
Hospital Benefits			
Maximum Days of Hospital Care	Days	Days	Days
Maximum Days for Mental Health or Substance Abuse	Days	Days	Days
Co-Pay If Yes, Amount of Co-Pay	☐ Yes ☐ No $	☐ Yes ☐ No $	☐ Yes ☐ No $
Annual Deductible If yes, Amount of Deductible	☐ Yes ☐ No $	☐ Yes ☐ No $	☐ Yes ☐ No $
Outpatient Care			
Emergency Room Care	☐ Yes ☐ No	☐ Yes ☐ No	☐ Yes ☐ No
Physical Therapy	☐ Yes ☐ No	☐ Yes ☐ No	☐ Yes ☐ No
Occupational Therapy	☐ Yes ☐ No	☐ Yes ☐ No	☐ Yes ☐ No
Speech Therapy	☐ Yes ☐ No	☐ Yes ☐ No	☐ Yes ☐ No
Dental Coverage	☐ Yes ☐ No	☐ Yes ☐ No	☐ Yes ☐ No
If Yes, Co-Pay for Regular Checkups	☐ Yes ☐ No	☐ Yes ☐ No	☐ Yes ☐ No
If Yes, Amount of Co-Pay	$	$	$
Orthodontic Coverage	☐ Yes ☐ No	☐ Yes ☐ No	☐ Yes ☐ No
If Yes, Co-Pay for Regular Checkups	☐ Yes ☐ No	☐ Yes ☐ No	☐ Yes ☐ No
If Yes, Amount of Co-Pay	$	$	$
Vision Coverage	☐ Yes ☐ No	☐ Yes ☐ No	☐ Yes ☐ No
Regular Eye Exam Frequency			
Co-Pay for Regular Eye Exams	$	$	$
Frequency for New Lenses			
Co-Pay for New Lenses	$	$	$
Frequency for New Frames			
Co-Pay for New Frames	$	$	$

1. Explain the differences you found in each plan (Indemnity Plan, HMO, and PPO).
2. Explain what planning for your health insurance needs has to do with protecting your wealth.

Name: ______________________

Date: ______________________

Insurance: Life & Health

OPEN RESPONSE #1

Please answer all parts of the question in the space provided.

Prompt: Jacob has begun working for a retail company that offers health insurance. He is trying to decide which plan is the best for him.

1. Jacob has asked you to explain what co-pay means and how this figures in his out-of-pocket expenses.
2. Explain to Jacob why comparing insurance costs is important to planning his budget.

Scoring Guide

- **4** Student gives correct answers for parts 1 and 2. All explanations are clear and complete. There is evidence of clear understanding of the concept.
- **3** Student gives correct answers for parts 1 and 2. Explanations are correct, but possibly unclear. There is less evidence of clear understanding.
- **2** Student answers 1 (1 or 2) part of the questions completely correct. There is some evidence of understanding.
- **1** Student gives only parts of correct answers. There is little evidence of understanding.
- **0** Response is totally incorrect or irrelevant (does not add any new information to the question).

Name: ______________________

Date: ______________________

CHAPTER 7

Insurance: Life & Health

OPEN RESPONSE #2

Please answer all parts of the question in the space provided.

Prompt: Adriana has just begun her first "real" job after graduating from college. Her new job offers several benefits. Along with health insurance, her new employer provides the option of purchasing low-cost life insurance. This will be the first time she has ever had to make a decision about purchasing life insurance. Her income at her new job is $42,000 a year and since she just graduated from college, she has no savings. She is not married but plans to marry in a year.

1. Explain to Adriana how to calculate how much life insurance coverage she might want to purchase at this time.
2. Calculate how much coverage she would need if she uses a multiple of 10 times her current income. Explain how you got your answer.

Scoring Guide

- **4** Student gives correct answers for parts 1 and 2. All explanations are clear and complete. There is evidence of clear understanding of the concept.
- **3** Student gives correct answers for parts 1 and 2. Explanations are correct, but possibly unclear. There is less evidence of clear understanding.
- **2** Student answers 1 (1 or 2) part of the questions completely correct. There is some evidence of understanding.
- **1** Student gives only parts of correct answers. There is little evidence of understanding.
- **0** Response is totally incorrect or irrelevant (does not add any new information to the question).

The Economy: Inflation and Growth

You will need the following math concepts in planning for your financial future. The first concept—**calculating inflation**—is useful for financial planning. Inflation, or a lasting increase in the general level of prices, cuts into our purchasing power. In other words, it reduces how far your money can go by increasing the number of dollars you need to buy goods and services.

The most common measure of inflation is the consumer price index (CPI). The CPI is a single number that is basically a weighted average of the prices of a market basket of about 300 goods and services consumed by the typical consumer. Food, entertainment, transportation, education and all other categories of goods and services are included in calculating the CPI.

How does the CPI work? The CPI number is based on a base year or period that changes from time to time. Today, the CPI is figured on the period of 1982–1984. The value of the market basket of goods and services from this base period is set at 100 and becomes the standard to which prices in later years are compared. For example, a CPI measure of 103 would indicate that it now costs $103 to buy goods and services that cost $100 in the base year. The 2011 CPI was 224.9. This indicates that $100 worth of goods and services bought in about 1983 now cost $224.90. As you can see, inflation forces us to spend more money to obtain the same benefit. With inflation, the income that used to purchase a certain amount of goods or services can no longer buy as much. In a real sense, the income is worth less even though it stays the same.

The second concept—**calculating economic growth**—is important because economic growth defines whether we are in a recession or in a growing economy. For this measure we use something called the real gross domestic product, or real GDP. The GDP is the total dollar value of all final goods and services produced domestically in a given year. The real GDP adjusts the measured GDP for inflation. If we did not use the real GDP, you might think the economy was growing or actually increasing output when in reality the change in GDP was merely the result of increasing prices. A growing real GDP is economic growth, or expansion, and means that the economy actually is producing more goods and services over the previous period. A shrinking real GDP is called a recession if it lasts for two consecutive quarters (six months). It is useful for us to understand these concepts because we hear a lot about them on the news. And, broad trends in the economy—growth or recession—may affect our economic decisions. For example, switching jobs or careers during an economic downturn may be a bad idea because new hires are often among the first let go when a company struggles.

Name: ____________________

Date: ____________________

CHAPTER 8

The Economy: Inflation and Growth

CONCEPT #1: Calculating Inflation

Remember that the most common measure of inflation is the consumer price index, or CPI. Therefore, we use changes in the CPI to get annual inflation rates. Let's look at an example. The CPI in 1985 was 107.6 and by the end of 1986 it was 109.6. What was the rate of inflation over that year? This calculation is essentially a rate of change. To calculate a rate of change, you use the following formula:

$$\text{Percent change} = (P_1 - P_0) \div P_0$$

where P_0 is the value in the original period and P_1 is the value in the next period. In this case P_0 = 107.6 and P_1 = 109.6. Therefore, the rate of change (inflation rate) is:

(109.6 – 107.6) ÷ 107.6 = .01859, which is approximately equal to 1.9 percent.

Math Review

(18.2 – 13.4) ÷ 13.4 = ________

(45.2 – 41.8) ÷ 41.8 = ________

(51.3 – 48.7) ÷ 48.7 = ________

45.36 × 1.1045 = ________

(123.4 – 112.6) ÷ 112.6 = ________

(181.4 – 171.5) ÷ 171.5 = ________

(149.1 – 146.7) ÷ 146.7 = ________

123.67 × 1.116 = ________

MyFinLitLab Apply Your Knowledge

1. In 1999 the CPI was 166.6. The CPI increased to 172.2 by 2000. What was the rate of inflation over that period?

2. In 1987 the CPI was 113.6. The CPI increased to 118.3 by 1988. What was the rate of inflation over that period?

3. In December 1979 the CPI was 76.9 The CPI increased to 86.4 by December 1980. What was the rate of inflation over that period?

4. Use the rate of inflation calculated from the previous question to answer this question. How much would a gallon of milk cost at the end of 1980 if a gallon of milk cost $1.15 in December 1979?

5. How much would the price of a $12,300 automobile increase over that same time period?

Name: ______________________

Date: ______________________

CHAPTER 8

The Economy: Inflation and Growth

CONCEPT #2: Calculating Economic Growth

Economic growth or decline (recession) is measured by changes in the real gross domestic product (GDP). Let's look at an example. In 1994 the real GDP (listed in billions of year 2000 dollars) was 7,835.4. In the following year of 1995 the real GDP was 8,031.7. How much did the economy grow during 1995?

This calculation is also essentially a rate of change. To calculate a rate of change you use the following formula:

$$\text{Percent change} = (P_1 - P_0) \div P_0$$

where P_0 is the value in the original period and P_1 is the value in the next period. In this case $P_0 = 7{,}835.4$ and $P_1 = 8{,}031.7$. The rate of change (growth rate) is therefore:

(8,031.7 – 7,835.4) ÷ 7,835.4 = .02505 which is approximately equal to 2.5 percent.

Math Review

(5,128.3 – 4,987.4) ÷ 4,987.4 = ________

(11,527.2 – 10,986.5) ÷ 10,986.5 = ________

(3,115.7 – 2,853.7) ÷ 2,853.7 = ________

(3,183.2 – 3,341.9) ÷ 3,341.9 = ________

(6,235.8 – 6,008.3) ÷ 6,008.3 = ________

(10,511.4 – 9,954.3) ÷ 9,954.3 = ________

(7,414.1 – 7,111.4) ÷ 7,111.4 = ________

(8,524.1 – 8,856.6) ÷ 8,856.6 = ________

MyFinLitLab **Apply Your Knowledge**

1. In 1999 the real GDP was 9,470.3. The real GDP increased to 9,817 by 2000. What was the rate of growth over that period?

2. In 1983 the real GDP was 5423.8. The real GDP increased to 5813.6 by 1984. What was the rate of growth over that period?

3. In 1990 the real GDP was 7,112.5. The real GDP decreased to 7,100.5 by 1991. What was the rate of growth over that period?

4. In 2002 the real GDP was 10048.8. The real GDP increased to 10301 by 2003. What was the rate of growth over that period?

5. In 2006 the real GDP was 11,319.4. The real GDP increased to 11,566.8 by 2007. What was the rate of growth over that period?

Name: ______________________

Date: ______________________

The Economy: Inflation and Growth

OPEN RESPONSE #1

Please answer all parts of the question in the space provided.

Prompt: Mario has come to you with questions about what he is reading in the newspaper. He is not sure he understands inflation. Mario has also asked you how it is calculated.

1. Explain to Mario inflation and what is the most common measure of inflation.
2. Explain to Mario how to calculate inflation or the rate of change.

Scoring Guide

4 Student gives correct answers for parts 1 and 2. All explanations are clear and complete. There is evidence of clear understanding of the concept.

3 Student gives correct answers for parts 1 and 2. Explanations are correct, but possibly unclear. There is less evidence of clear understanding.

2 Student answers 1 (1 or 2) part of the questions completely correct. There is some evidence of understanding.

1 Student gives only parts of correct answers. There is little evidence of understanding.

0 Response is totally incorrect or irrelevant (does not add any new information to the question).

Name: ______________________

Date: ______________________

The Economy: Inflation and Growth

OPEN RESPONSE #2

Please answer all parts of the question in the space provided.

Prompt: Anisha heard about the GDP in her Economics class. She knows this is an important concept but has come to you for more information.

1. Explain to Anisha why knowing the real GDP (gross domestic product) is important to her financial plan.
2. Explain to Anisha how to calculate economic growth.

Scoring Guide

- **4** Student gives correct answers for parts 1 and 2. All explanations are clear and complete. There is evidence of clear understanding of the concept.
- **3** Student gives correct answers for parts 1 and 2. Explanations are correct, but possibly unclear. There is less evidence of clear understanding.
- **2** Student answers 1 (1 or 2) part of the questions completely correct. There is some evidence of understanding.
- **1** Student gives only parts of correct answers. There is little evidence of understanding.
- **0** Response is totally incorrect or irrelevant (does not add any new information to the question).

Credit Calculations

You can use the following math concepts in planning for your financial future. The first concept—**calculating the cost of a credit purchase**—can help you understand what an item is actually costing you if you finance it. The people who sell consumer durable goods, such as furniture, appliances, and entertainment systems, often have easy financing available. However, on closer inspection of the fine print, you may determine that the terms for this financing include very high rates of interest. In order to evaluate the real cost of an item, you need to consider the financing costs.

The second concept—**calculating potential interest on zero interest teaser offers**—is useful to help you make purchasing decisions. Vendors may use a number of techniques to attract potential buyers. Sometimes you will see zero interest deals in which the seller will finance an item for some period of time with no interest charges. Often, if the item is not paid in full by that time, the interest will be charged retroactively. In other words, if you fail to pay off the item quickly, you may find that you owe the cost of the item plus all the interest that would have accrued during the "zero interest" period.

Name: ____________________

Date: ____________________

CHAPTER 9

Credit Calculations

CONCEPT #1: Calculating the Cost of a Credit Purchase

How much does something truly cost if we finance it? Sometimes consumers are tempted to buy an item before they might normally purchase the item simply because it is on sale. Yet, very often they turn around and finance the purchase using a costly source of credit. So, how much did the purchase really cost? This exercise will help you make those comparisons of cash purchase versus credit purchase.

For example, let's assume you bought $2,500 worth of furniture on sale and financed it for 24 months at the store's interest rate of 18 percent annually with payments of $124.81 per month. When you figure the actual amount you wound up paying for the furniture, you find that it was $124.81 × 24 = $2,995.44, which is $495.44 more than the original $2,500 purchase price.

Math Review

24(123.45) – 2,500 = ________ (30 × 167.34) – 4,000 = ________

36(237.73) – 6,400 = ________ (48 × 202.11) – 8,000 = ________

18(67.31) – 1,000 = ________ (60 × 111.38) – 5,000 = ________

42(112.98) – 3,500 = ________ (54 × 231.65) – 9,000 = ________

MyFinLitLab **Apply Your Knowledge**

1. How much in interest will Jamison pay for a 36-month $3,000 loan that charges 10 percent interest? The payments will be $96.80 per month.

2. Salinda borrowed $4,200 to buy some furniture. Her monthly payments over four years with an interest rate of 24 percent are $136.93 per month. How much in total interest will she pay?

3. Jesse is thinking about buying an entertainment system that will cost $1,800. The store will finance the purchase for 12 months at 20 percent interest. His payments will be $166.74. How much will he pay in interest over the life of the loan?

4. Quantrell bought a television set on sale for his apartment for $1,500, but he will spread the payments over two years. The store charges 18 percent interest for financing, and his payments will be $74.89. How much will he pay in interest over the life of the loan?

5. Ava's payments on her new furniture will be $162.88 per month for 60 months. Assuming the furniture cost $7,000 on sale, how much will she pay in interest by the time her loan is paid in full?

Name: ______________________

Date: ______________________

Credit Calculations

CONCEPT #2: Calculating Potential Interest on Zero Interest Teaser Offers

One common method of increasing sales is to entice buyers to purchase the product now on credit and have a period of time where there are no interest charges. Buyers who pay the debt in full prior to the expiration of this period will incur no interest costs. However, buyers who are unable to pay the amount owed before the zero-interest period expires often discover that interest is then charged beginning from the time of purchase. For example, what if you bought $1,000 worth of furniture on a program that said "90 days, same as cash"? If you paid the amount in full prior to the end of the 90-day period, you would only pay $1,000. However, if you waited until 91 days and exceeded the zero-interest period, you would have to pay interest on the entire amount for the full 91 days. Assuming the interest rate is 18 percent annually, you would have to pay for three months worth of interest. You would pay ((.18 ÷ 12)(3 months)) × $1,000 = $45 in interest charges for that period of time. In reality, the company may also use monthly compounding, so the interest charges could be slightly higher.

Math Review

(.24 ÷ 12)(6) × $4,000 = ________

(.22 ÷ 12)(4) × $2,200 = ________

(.18 ÷ 12)(3) × $1,600 = ________

(.19 ÷ 12)(2) × $2,700 = ________

(.21 ÷ 12)(4) × $1,800 = ________

(.23 ÷ 12)(2) × $3,850 = ________

(.24 ÷ 12)(6) × $2,354 = ________

(.17 ÷ 12)(5) × $1,559 = ________

MyFinLitLab Apply Your Knowledge

1. Jeffrey bought $1,500 worth of furniture on credit using a "90 days, same as cash" offer at a local store. How much interest will he pay if he goes 91 days before he pays the bill in full assuming the annual interest rate is 24 percent?

2. Calista purchased an entertainment center for $2,200 with a zero-interest option if the account was paid in full in 60 days. Assuming she did not pay the $2,200 until 90 days, how much interest did she have to pay in addition to the $2,200 if the interest rate converted to an 18 percent annual rate?

3. Micah paid $3,100 for a new living room set and does not have to pay any interest if she pays the balance within six months. However, if she goes 1 day beyond six months, she will have to pay interest on the entire time period at an annual rate of 21 percent. How much interest will she owe if she goes 1 day beyond six months to pay the bill?

4. Jeremiah bought a new keyboard that cost $2,400. The store offered a "six months same as cash" deal that charges 22 percent interest if he goes past the six-month period prior to paying the debt. How much will the interest be if he doesn't pay for eight months?

5. Yari charged $1,600 at the local sporting goods store. She will not have to pay interest if she pays the balance in full in 90 days. After that time she will have to pay 24 percent annual interest on the amount for the entire period. How much interest will she owe if she waits 105 days to pay the bill?

Name: ______________________

Date: ______________________

Credit Calculations

OPEN RESPONSE #1

Please answer all parts of the question in the space provided.

Prompt: Carlos wants a new entertainment unit (cabinet, system, the works) but he only has $350 for a down payment on the $3,500 unit. He is going to finance the remaining amount. The store offers him an in-store finance program for 36 months with an interest rate of 24 percent annually. His payments will be $123.58 per month.

1. Calculate the amount of interest Carlos will pay. Show or explain how you got your answer.

2. Explain to Carlos the actual cost of the new entertainment unit once it is paid off compared to the actual cost of the unit.

Scoring Guide

4 Student gives correct answers for parts 1 and 2. All explanations are clear and complete. There is evidence of clear understanding of the concept.

3 Student gives correct answers for parts 1 and 2. Explanations are correct, but possibly unclear. There is less evidence of clear understanding.

2 Student answers 1 (1 or 2) part of the questions completely correct. There is some evidence of understanding.

1 Student gives only parts of correct answers. There is little evidence of understanding.

0 Response is totally incorrect or irrelevant (does not add any new information to the question).

Name: ______________________

Date: ______________________

CHAPTER 9

Credit Calculations

OPEN RESPONSE #2

Please answer all parts of the question in the space provided.

Prompt: Jocelyn has moved into her first apartment. There is a sofa at the furniture store she really wants for her new apartment. It cost $800, but all she has right now is $150. She wants to finance the remainder using the store's 90-day zero interest offer. If she does not pay off the remainder before the end of the 90 days, she will be charged 21 percent interest.

1. Explain to Jocelyn how this type of program works. Be sure to point out the advantage(s) and disadvantage(s) of this type of program.
2. Calculate the interest Jocelyn will pay if she waits until day 91 to pay off her sofa. Show or explain how you got your answer.

Scoring Guide

4 Student gives correct answers for parts 1 and 2. All explanations are clear and complete. There is evidence of clear understanding of the concept.

3 Student gives correct answers for parts 1 and 2. Explanations are correct, but possibly unclear. There is less evidence of clear understanding.

2 Student answers 1 (1 or 2) part of the questions completely correct. There is some evidence of understanding.

1 Student gives only parts of correct answers. There is little evidence of understanding.

0 Response is totally incorrect or irrelevant (does not add any new information to the question).

CHAPTER 10

Personal Loans: Houses and Cars

You can use the following math concepts in planning for your financial future. The first concept—**calculating interest paid**—is useful to help you see the real cost of buying a home or any other asset. Not only do you pay the negotiated price of the asset, you must also pay interest on the money you borrow to buy the asset. Calculating interest paid helps us put borrowing money into perspective. It costs money to borrow money, and borrowing should be reserved for major purchases.

The second concept—**calculating the down payment**—is useful when buying any big-ticket item that requires a down payment. Down payments are most often expressed as a percentage of the purchase price. It therefore requires simple calculations to determine how much you will need to save in order to buy a specific asset such as a car, truck, or house.

The third concept—**calculating the amount you can borrow using home equity**—is useful for many homeowners who have built equity in their homes. Equity is the difference between what you owe on the house and what the house is truly worth. When you build equity in a home, you have an asset you can borrow against. These home equity loans are a popular source of relatively low-interest credit that some people may elect to use for home repairs, renovations, and, sometimes, debt consolidation.

Name: ____________________

Date: ____________________

CHAPTER 10

Personal Loans: Houses and Cars

CONCEPT #1: Calculating Interest Paid

When you finance any item and pay for it over a period of time, each payment will include the interest charged to that point and some amount that will reduce the principal. Therefore, every payment you make reduces the original amount of the loan until the loan is paid in full. Depending on the interest rate and the length of the loan, you will see that the interest payments can easily add up to a sizable amount—sometimes even more than the amount of the original loan. Knowing this fact may cause you to begin to save and earn interest on your money in order to avoid having to borrow to make some purchases.

Let's look at an example. Let's assume you are borrowing $150,000 to buy a house. The loan terms are an 8 percent interest rate financed for 30 years. Under these terms, you will make monthly payments of $1,100.65 for 30 years. How much in interest will you pay over this period of time?

$1,100.65 × 360 months = $396,234 in total that you will pay for this house—on top of any down payment. Since the original amount borrowed was $150,000, you can subtract that amount from the total payments to get the amount of interest paid over the life of the loan. So, $396,234 – $150,000 = $246,234 in interest.

Math Review

(180 × 558.24) – 65,000 = ________

(180 × 235.67) – 22,000 = ________

(180 × 1,536.51) – 150,000 = ________

(180 × 851.43) – 115,000 = ________

(360 × 1,118.32) – 250,000 = ________

(360 × 2,234.39) – 500,000 = ________

(360 × 1,219.56) – 250,000 = ________

(360 × 884.61) – 200,000 = ________

MyFinLitLab **Apply Your Knowledge**

1. How much interest will you pay over the life of a $150,000 15-year loan at 7 percent interest with monthly payments of $1,348.24?

2. How much interest will you pay over the life of a $125,000 15-year loan at 6 percent with monthly payments of $1,054.82?

3. How much interest will you pay over the life of a $200,000 15-year loan at 5 percent with monthly payments of $1,581.59?

4. How much interest will you pay over the life of a $220,000 30-year loan at 8 percent with monthly payments of $1,614.28?

5. How much interest will you pay over the life of a $150,000 30-year loan at 7 percent with monthly payments of $997.95?

Name: ______________________

Date: ______________________

Personal Loans: Houses and Cars

CONCEPT #2: Calculating the Down Payment

Many major purchases, such as autos, motorcycles, boats, and houses, require a down payment. The most common way that down payments are expressed is using a percent of the sale price. For example, in order to buy a car for $18,000 you may have to pay 10 percent of the purchase price as a down payment. In this case you express the percent as a decimal and simply multiply $18,000 × .10 = $1,800 needed for the down payment. The amount financed would therefore be equal to $18,000 – $1,800 = $16,200.

Math Review

78,000 × .05 = ________	11,500 × .10 = ________	23,000 × .20 = ________
150,000 × .05 = ________	24,200 × .10 = ________	34,000 × .20 = ________
220,000 × .05 = ________	31,800 × .10 = ________	41,000 × .20 = ________
97,500 × .05 = ________	23,740 × .10 = ________	129,500 × .20 = ________

MyFinLitLab **Apply Your Knowledge**

1. Jason is buying a car priced at $15,000 that requires a down payment of 15 percent. How much money does he need to come up with?

2. Linda needs to come up with a 10 percent down payment on a house priced at $127,400. How much money does she need to have saved?

3. Kimber is thinking about buying a four-wheeler that is priced at $6,700. However, he needs 20 percent down in order to finance it. How much money does he need?

4. Kendra is looking at a car that will cost $11,500. She needs to come up with a 15 percent down payment to get more favorable financing terms. How much will she need for this down payment?

5. Ramik is buying a house for $223,000 that requires a 5 percent down payment. How much money will he need for the down payment?

Name: ____________________

Date: ____________________

Personal Loans: Houses and Cars

CONCEPT #3: Calculating the Amount You Can Borrow Using Home Equity

Home equity loans are a popular source of financing for many people. People who have accumulated equity in their home either by paying their original mortgage down or through home price appreciation may elect to use that equity as collateral for a loan. These home equity loans allow homeowners to borrow up to some percentage of the equity in their home. For example, you may have a home that has an appraised value of $200,000 on which you still owe $124,000 on the original mortgage. Your bank offers home equity loans that will allow you to borrow up to 80 percent of the equity in your home. How much can you borrow? First you have to determine the equity amount—the difference between what your home is worth and what you owe on it. In this example, your equity is $200,000 – $124,000 = $76,000. If you can borrow up to 80 percent of this amount, you can borrow $76,000 × .80 = $60,800.

Math Review

(140,000 – 112,000) × .80 = ________

(180,000 – 54,000) × .90 = ________

(135,000 – 86,000) × .80 = ________

(276,000 – 155,000) × .90 = ________

(223,000 – 184,000) × .75 = ________

(320,000 – 221,000) × .95 = ________

(189,500 – 124,300) × .80 = ________

(100,500 – 72,000) × .75 = ________

MyFinLitLab **Apply Your Knowledge**

1. Greta wants to take out a home equity loan on her house. She owes $37,000 on her mortgage, but her house is worth about $125,000. She can borrow up to 80 percent of her equity. How much can she borrow?

2. Zeke still owes $145,000 on his home which is worth about $225,000. How much could he borrow against his equity if he can borrow up to 90 percent?

3. Brandon has a home valued at $235,000 that he owes $180,000 on the first mortgage. How much can he borrow against his equity if he takes out a 90 percent equity loan?

4. Aliyah has a home mortgage of $225,000. However, her home is worth $345,000. How much can she borrow using an 80 percent home equity loan?

5. Kalia can borrow up to 90 percent of the equity in her home. She owes $124,000 on a home that is worth $234,000. How much can she borrow?

Name: ____________________

Date: ____________________

Personal Loans: Houses and Cars

OPEN RESPONSE #1

Please answer all parts of the question in the space provided.

Prompt: Samantha has found a great condo that she is sure she can afford. The condo sells for $149,500. She is trying to determine if she has enough saved at this time for a down payment on the condo.

1. Calculate Samantha's down payment if she needs to pay 20 percent of the total cost of the condo. Show or explain how you got your answer.

2. Calculate the amount Samantha will be financing if she purchases the condo. Show or explain how you got your answer.

Scoring Guide

4 Student gives correct answers for parts 1 and 2. All explanations are clear and complete. There is evidence of clear understanding of the concept.

3 Student gives correct answers for parts 1 and 2. Explanations are correct, but possibly unclear. There is less evidence of clear understanding.

2 Student answers 1 (1 or 2) part of the questions completely correct. There is some evidence of understanding.

1 Student gives only parts of correct answers. There is little evidence of understanding.

0 Response is totally incorrect or irrelevant (does not add any new information to the question).

Name: ____________________

Date: ____________________

Personal Loans: Houses and Cars

OPEN RESPONSE #2

Please answer all parts of the question in the space provided.

Prompt: Contessa has found a small home in the neighborhood where she grew up that she would like to buy. It is an older home and she will need to do some remodeling later. Right now she wants to finance $112,000 at 8 percent for the house. Her payment will be $821.82 for 30 years.

1. Calculate the total amount Contessa will pay for the house at the end of 30 years. Show or explain how you got your answer.

2. Calculate the amount of interest Contessa will pay over the life of the loan. Show or explain how you got your answer.

Scoring Guide

4 Student gives correct answers for parts 1 and 2. All explanations are clear and complete. There is evidence of clear understanding of the concept.

3 Student gives correct answers for parts 1 and 2. Explanations are correct, but possibly unclear. There is less evidence of clear understanding.

2 Student answers 1 (1 or 2) part of the questions completely correct. There is some evidence of understanding.

1 Student gives only parts of correct answers. There is little evidence of understanding.

0 Response is totally incorrect or irrelevant (does not add any new information to the question).

Credit Cards

You can use the following math concepts in planning for your financial future. The first concept—**approximating credit card interest charges**—is useful for two reasons. One, we can use it to see how costly it can be to buy things on credit and not pay in full every month. Second, it can help us make sure there are no errors on our monthly statement. It is common to find that there is an error on your credit card bill. If you do not catch the error and call the company, the chances are high that it will go undetected and cost you money.

The second concept—**calculating the true cost of ATM fees**—is a useful exercise that helps you understand just how costly it can be to utilize cash advances on your credit card. These withdrawals are not subject to the typical no-interest grace period, and in addition there are high fees associated with withdrawal.

The third concept—**keeping track of your card balance—**is useful because it may help you avoid overdraft charges or the embarrassment of having your card denied for some purchase. Remember, you credit card has a limit, and if you exceed that limit you will either pay an overdraft fee or your purchase will be refused.

Name: ____________________

Date: ____________________

Credit Cards

CONCEPT #1: Approximating Credit Card Interest Charges

Credit cards commonly charge high rates of interest that can be more than 20 percent annually. In addition, credit cards compound interest daily. Compounding is the process of charging interest on interest. In daily compounding, the company calculates the interest at the end of the day and adds it to the amount owed. The next day's interest is a little higher since the amount owed is the sum of the original amount plus the previous day's interest charges. This process continues to add slightly higher interest charges to your balance every day. While daily compounding amounts to a lot of money for a large credit card company with millions of accounts, it really makes a minor difference in your monthly bill. When it comes to approximating interest charges, you can simply take the annual interest rate, divide by 12 to get a monthly interest rate, and then multiply that rate by the monthly account balance. Because this does not factor in daily compounding, this calculation will not give you the precise interest charges you will owe. But it will come close—close enough to see that it would be much better to pay your account in full every month rather than carry a balance on a high-interest rate credit card.

Let's assume you owe $1,000 on your credit card from the previous month and your card charges an annual rate of 18 percent. Approximately how much should this month's interest charge be for the $1,000 balance on your statement?

$$.18 \div 12 = .015 \text{ per month} \times \$1{,}000 = \$15$$

Note: Since your credit card compounds interest daily the amount would actually be slightly higher than this amount. However, if the amount differs greatly you should contact the company to see if they have made a mistake.

Math Review

$(.18 \div 12) \times 767 =$ ________

$(.21 \div 12) \times 1{,}500 =$ ________

$(.19 \div 12) \times 1{,}000 =$ ________

$(.22 \div 12) \times 3{,}400 =$ ________

$(.18 \div 12) \times 4{,}500 =$ ________

$(.21 \div 12) \times 8{,}400 =$ ________

$(.21 \div 12) \times 6{,}171 =$ ________

$(.20 \div 12) \times 8{,}511 =$ ________

$(.19 \div 12) \times 2{,}120 =$ ________

$(.24 \div 12) \times 4{,}487 =$ ________

$(.16 \div 12) \times 5{,}109 =$ ________

$(.15 \div 12) \times 1{,}425 =$ ________

MyFinLitLab Apply Your Knowledge

1. Approximately how much interest will accrue before next month's bill if Jill owes $4,500 on her credit card and it charges 21 percent annually?

2. Approximately how much interest will Karen owe on her credit card next month if the balance she carried over from the previous month was $2,450 and her annual interest rate is 18 percent?

3. Bryson owes $5,184 on his credit card that charges 22 percent annually. About how much will his next month's interest charge be?

4. Kiera still owes $450 on her credit card from the previous month. Her annual interest rate is 18 percent. Approximately how much should the interest charges be when she gets her bill?

5. Ralston charged a $2,400 couch on his credit card and still owes $2,200 on the remaining balance. Assuming his card charges 24 percent annual interest, how much will his interest charge be next month?

Name: ____________________

Date: ____________________

Credit Cards

CONCEPT #2: Calculating the True Cost of ATM Fees

Most credit cards offer the opportunity to get cash advances, but typically charge a fee of $1 to $3 for this transaction. Sometimes the fees are even expressed as a percentage of the advance, such as 1 or 2 percent. In addition, automated teller machines, or ATMs, also charge similar fees for these cash advances. And, cash advances immediately begin accruing interest without having a grace period. Because of these fees, cash advances are an extremely expensive source of financing. Let's look at an example. Assume you got a $50 cash advance from an ATM. The ATM company charged a $2 fee and the credit card company charged another $2 fee. In addition, your credit card charges a 24 percent annual rate on cash advances. Assuming only monthly compounding for simplicity, how much did this advance cost you for 30 days?

$50 + $2 + $2 = $54 charged on your credit card for the $50 advance

At 2 percent per month, the interest charges were an additional $54 × .02 = $1.08. Therefore, you paid a total of $1.08 + $2 + $2 = $5.08 for a $50 advance. As a percentage this amount represents approximately 10 percent interest for one month. ($5.08 ÷ $50 = .1016 or 10.16 percent for the month). A very rough approximation for an annual rate would be to multiply that 10.16 percent × 12 months = 122 percent.

Math Review

(200 × .04) + 3 = ________ (150 × .03) + 2 = ________

(340 × .02) + 1.50 = ________ (50 × .04) + 1.50 = ________

(220 × .03) + 4 = ________ (75 × .02) + 3 = ________

(100 × .04) + 2.50 = ________ (180 × .03) + 2.50 = ________

MyFinLitLab **Apply Your Knowledge**

1. Justin got a $100 cash advance on his credit card. The credit card company charges a 3 percent fee and the ATM charged $2. How much did his cash advance cost him in fees?

2. What is the approximate annual percentage rate assuming he paid the amount in full in 30 days and the cash advance interest rate on his credit card is 18 percent?

3. Kim got a $40 advance on her credit card at the ATM. She was charged $1.50 for an ATM fee and $2 by her credit card company for the advance. Approximately what annual percentage interest rate is she paying in fees for this advance assuming she pays the bill in 20 days?

4. Landry took out a cash advance of $200 on his credit card. If the bank charges him a $3 fee and his credit card company charges 3 percent of the advance, how much did the advance cost him?

5. What approximate annual percentage rate is that, ignoring any interest charges assuming Landry paid in full in 30 days?

Name: ____________________

Date: ____________________

CHAPTER 11

Credit Cards

CONCEPT #3: Keeping Track of Your Card Balance

When you use your credit card for convenience purchases, it is often easy to lose track of how much money you have charged. If you have a card with a low credit limit or one that you are carrying a balance on that is near the credit limit, you might find yourself paying an overdraft fee—or in cases where you do not have overdraft protection, having your charge denied. Keep a small ledger or notepad handy and write down your charges so you can keep track of your total. For example, how much do you owe on a card on which you charged two tanks of gas for \$56.76 and \$45.42 and one meal of \$15.23? Simply add the charges up; \$56.76 + \$45.42 + \$15.23 = \$117.41. Knowing how much you owe can keep you from overspending.

Math Review

12.56 + 124.76 + 96.32 = ________

76.23 + 568.41 + 88.75 = ________

32.11 + 411.59 + 91.28 = ________

17.19 + 258.22 + 44.21 = ________

334.87 + 44.21 +1,008.21 = ________

513.67 + 51.14 + 2,562.24 = ________

981.28 + 11.54 + 1,287.52 = ________

774.16 + 73.37 + 1,745.82 = ________

MyFinLitLab **Apply Your Knowledge**

1. Jessi charged \$32 on her credit card for some clothes, \$45.95 to fill up her tank with gas, and \$14.95 for pizza. What was the total amount of her charges?

2. Rashawnda had to do some shopping for the holidays. She spent \$123.21 at one store, \$35.76 at a second store, and \$322.72 at the last place. How much did she charge in total?

3. Clayton had to charge some school clothes on his credit card. He spent \$44.22, \$67.53, and \$176.11 to replenish his wardrobe. How much did he charge in total?

4. Kristoph charged \$512.41 on his credit card for some tools he needed for work. He also filled up his truck with gas and charged another \$55.25 on the same card. One week later he filled up his truck again and charged another \$42.11 for gas. How much did he charge in total?

5. Lazrus used his credit card to buy a pair of shoes for \$123.76 and a tank of gas for \$38.52. How much were his total charges?

Name: ______________________

Date: ______________________

Credit Cards

OPEN RESPONSE #1

Please answer all parts of the question in the space provided.

Prompt: Julia needed cash fast. She wanted to go to the movies and dinner with friends. She knew that she was able to get a cash advance on her credit card, so she found an ATM where she could get a $60 cash advance. The ATM charged her $2.50 for the transaction. When she got her credit card bill 30 days later, she saw that the credit card company charged her $3.00 for the transaction. She was also charged interest on the withdrawal of 2.25 percent per month.

1. Calculate the amount of cost to Julia for her night out. Show or explain how you got your answer.

2. Explain to Julia why her evening was so expensive. What could she have done to save some money?

Scoring Guide

4 Student gives correct answers for parts 1 and 2. All explanations are clear and complete. There is evidence of clear understanding of the concept.

3 Student gives correct answers for parts 1 and 2. Explanations are correct, but possibly unclear. There is less evidence of clear understanding.

2 Student answers 1 (1 or 2) part of the questions completely correct. There is some evidence of understanding.

1 Student gives only parts of correct answers. There is little evidence of understanding.

0 Response is totally incorrect or irrelevant (does not add any new information to the question).

Name: ____________________

Date: ____________________

CHAPTER 11

Credit Cards

OPEN RESPONSE #2

Please answer all parts of the question in the space provided.

Prompt: Emery was never sure how much he had charged on his gas credit card each month. It was always shocking to him when he got the bill. For instance, one month he had charged two tanks of gas for $43.50 and $33.80, purchased snacks at the local station for $3.18, $5.34, and $8.93, and bought a quart of oil for his car at $6.49. When the bill arrived he had no idea he owed so much.

1. Explain to Emery what he could do to help him keep track of his spending on the credit card. Explain to Emery why it is important to keep up with his spending on the credit card.
2. Calculate what Emery spent in one month using his gas credit card. Show or explain how you got your answer.

Scoring Guide

4 Student gives correct answers for parts 1 and 2. All explanations are clear and complete. There is evidence of clear understanding of the concept.

3 Student gives correct answers for parts 1 and 2. Explanations are correct, but possibly unclear. There is less evidence of clear understanding.

2 Student answers 1 (1 or 2) part of the questions completely correct. There is some evidence of understanding.

1 Student gives only parts of correct answers. There is little evidence of understanding.

0 Response is totally incorrect or irrelevant (does not add any new information to the question).

CHAPTER 12

Banking

You can use the following math concepts in planning for your financial future. The first concept—**keeping track of checking account balances**—is useful to keep from overdrawing your account. With the widespread use of debit cards, which allows for immediate withdrawal of checking-account funds—it is becoming easier to lose track of how much money you have in the bank. However, overdraft charges and bounced check fees associated with overdrawn accounts make this a costly mistake.

The second concept—**calculating the cost of a bounced check**—is useful to see just how expensive it is to lose track of your account balance. When you bounce a check, not only does the bank charge a non-sufficient funds fee, but the vendor will charge a fee as well. This exercise will help you see just how expensive a bounced check can be.

The third concept—**balancing your checking account**—is necessary to ensure that neither you nor the bank make errors in figuring your checking account balance. Even if you faithfully record deposits and checks, it is possible for errors—yours or the bank's—to occur. To discover these errors as quickly as possible, you should regularly compare your records to the bank's. This process is known as balancing or reconciling your account.

Name: ______________________

Date: ______________________

CHAPTER 12

Banking

CONCEPT #1: Keeping Track of Checking Account Balances

Keeping track of your checking account balance can be challenging, particularly if you share an account with another person. Sometimes one or both of you may forget to record a purchase or withdrawal in the ledger. As a result. the balance shown will be higher than the amount you actually have available. Debit cards also make it easy to make mistakes, since we often carry our debit card and do not have our checking account ledger with us. This increases the likelihood of making a withdrawal and then forgetting to record it. Try to make a habit of recording purchases and withdrawals, subtracting those amounts and any fees from your account balance, and adding any deposits so that you can keep an accurate tally and avoid overdrawing your account.

Math Review

500 – 23.41 – 56.74 – 11.15 + 100 = ________

1,000 – 327.45 – 211.23 – 76.43 – 50 + 455.67 = ________

895.54 + 125 + 45 – 511.89 – 112.62 – 200 = ________

241.03 – 179.36 + 554.11 – 126.98 – 25.36 – 89.74 = ________

MyFinLitLab Apply Your Knowledge

1. Beatrice's account had a $245 balance before she deposited her paycheck of $221.31. She then wrote checks for $23.75, $89.57, and $55.98. She also withdrew $40 cash using her debit card? What is her new balance?

2. Jericho withdrew $100 using his debit card. He also debited $12.15 and $25.67 at the mall. Assuming he started with an account balance of $250, how much does he have in his account now?

3. Mareid deposited her $236.75 paycheck into her checking account. Her previous balance was $331.63. She also debited $45.87 and $15.25 on that same day. How much does she have in her account now?

4. Felicia's account balance showed $455.25 before she debited $42.18, $194.56, and $211.23. How much does she have in her account now?

5. Bracy's checking account balance showed $578.21. However, he deposited a check of $225 and wrote two checks for $231.87 and $48.71 respectively. How much does he have in his account now?

Name: ____________________

Date: ____________________

CHAPTER 12

Banking

CONCEPT #2: Calculating the Cost of a Bounced Check

Losing track of your checking account balance can result in a bounced check—a check returned for non-sufficient funds (NSF). This occurs when a merchant presents your check to your bank and you do not have enough money in your account to cover the check. If this occurs, the merchant will contact you for the original payment and also charge you a fee that in most cases will range from $20 to $30. Your bank will also assess a charge for the NSF check—typically $20 to $30. In some cases you may have overdraft protection at your bank, in which case the bank will cover the check and the merchant will receive his or her money. However, you likely will still be assessed the bank's overdraft fee.

For example, assume you wrote a check for $41.15 and your account balance was only $32. The bank would not honor this check. It would return it to the merchant as an NSF check. The merchant would then charge you a fee—say, $25. Your bank will also charge a fee—let's say $30. What is the total cost of this purchase? $41.15 + $25 + $30 = $96.15. As you can see, this is a very expensive mistake to make.

Keep in mind also that it is not uncommon for a person to write several checks at once. Each may be subject to merchant and bank charges.

Math Review

$21.19 + $25 + $30 = ________

$55.56 + $25 + $30 = ________

$45.11 + $30 + $30 = ________

$178.61 + $25 + $35 = ________

$72.31 + $25 + $25 = ________

$112.98 + $25 + $25 = ________

$451.21 + $25 + $30 = ________

$311.23 + $25 + $30 = ________

MyFinLitLab

Apply Your Knowledge

1. Hanna wrote a check for $12.31 and did not have enough money in her account to cover the check. She was charged $25 by the merchant and another $25 by the bank for an NSF check. How much did that purchase actually cost her?

2. Naim bought a T-shirt for $25.50. He knew there wasn't enough money in his account, but he believed he could get to the bank and make a deposit in time to cover it. However, he did not make the deposit in time and was charged a $30 NSF fee by the bank and a $35 bounced check fee by the T-shirt vendor. How much did the shirt actually cost him?

3. Owen paid $11.50 for a pizza and bounced a check. His bank paid the check because he had overdraft protection but charged him a $20 fee. How much did the pizza cost him?

4. Karlin bought some clothes at the mall and bounced two checks; one for $32.54 and another for $27.87. Assuming the stores each charged a $25 NSF fee and his bank charges $20 per bounced check, how much did he spend in total for the clothes?

5. How much would Karlin have spent on the clothes had he not bounced the checks?

Name: ____________________

Date: ____________________

CHAPTER 12

Banking

CONCEPT #3: Balancing Your Checking Account

Balancing your account is a method used to make sure you have the correct balance in your checking account. Why is it important to balance your checkbook? You may forget to record a debit or check. You may write the check amount down improperly or incorrectly subtract the amount of a check from your balance. You may be assessed a fee by the bank that you do not record or even know about. Or, the bank could make an error in your account. All of these are possible sources of error that could lead you to believe you have more in your checking account than you actually have—which can lead to bounced checks. There are a number of reasons you should balance your checking account.

Once a month, the bank will send you a bank statement. This statement lists the bank's records of all the deposits and checks written against your account. The statement will also give you an account balance—the amount of money the bank recognizes as being in your account. When you receive this statement you need to reconcile, or match up, the bank's balance with the balance recorded in your ledger. It is helpful to use a separate sheet of paper, divided into two columns, for this exercise. One column represents the bank statement balance. The other represents your checkbook register balance—the amount your records indicate are in your account.

Step 1. In one column, write the balance given on the statement.

Step 2. To the balance, add any recent deposits that you have made to the account that do not appear on the bank statement.

Step 3. From this total, subtract any ATM withdrawals you have made from your checking account and the amount of any checks that you have written that do not appear on the statement. These would include withdrawals and checks you wrote in the last couple of days, after the statement was prepared and mailed to your home. It may also include checks you wrote awhile ago that the recipient for some reason has not yet cashed. The amount represented by these outstanding checks is likely to be taken from your account at any moment, when the checks are presented for payment.

The total you have after completing Steps 1–3 is the reconciled bank balance.

Step 4. Now, move to the other column on your sheet. There, record the balance listed in your checkbook register. This is the amount you believe you have right now.

Step 5. To this amount, add any interest earned by your account, and deduct any fees your bank has charged you in the last month. These amounts should be listed in your bank statement.

Step 6. Compare the final total of Steps 1–3 with the total from Steps 4–5. They should be the same. If the amounts are not equal, you need to track down the mistake. It may be a math error on your part or it could be an error on the bank's part. It could also be that your forgot to write down a check you wrote or an ATM withdrawal you made. Or, you may have written the amount down wrong.

Let's look at an example. Assume the bank statement shows your balance as $523.87, yet your checkbook register balance shows a balance of $419.45. However, you also notice that you deposited a check last night in the night deposit box for $250 that is not reflected in the bank's statement. You also have written two checks that have not posted at the bank yet. One check was for $128.52 and the other for $231.90. In addition, the bank charged you a $6 monthly service charge on your account that is not recorded in your ledger. If we plug the numbers into the following form, we will see that our reconciled balances match. As long as these numbers match we have no errors.

Bank Statement Balance	**$523.87**	**Checkbook Register Balance**	**$419.45**
Plus Deposits in Transit (*Total any checks that you have written that do not appear on the bank statement. Use the following worksheet to aid your computations.*)	$250.00	Plus Interest	$
Minus Outstanding Checks (*Total any checks that you have written that do not appear on the bank statement.*)	$128.52 $231.90	Minus Service Charge	$6
Reconciled Balance	$413.45	Reconciled Balance	$413.45

Now, fill one out with these numbers. Your bank statement shows a balance of $1,311.23 and your checkbook ledger shows a balance of $1,598.12. However, you note that you have recorded two deposits that are not on the bank's statement—one for $500 and another for $128. You also have written three checks for $222.34, $45.98, and $71.78, respectively, that have not cleared the bank. You do not have a service charge this month since your account balance was high enough and you earned $1.01 in interest.

Bank Statement Balance	$	**Checkbook Register Balance**	$
Plus Deposits in Transit (*Total any checks that you have written that do not appear on the bank statement. Use the following worksheet to aid your computations.*)	$ $	Plus Interest	$
Minus Outstanding Checks (*Total any checks that you have written that do not appear on the bank statement.*)	$ $ $	Minus Service Charge	$
Reconciled Balance	$	Reconciled Balance	$

Name: ______________________

Date: ______________________

CHAPTER 12

Banking

OPEN RESPONSE #1

Please answer all parts of the question in the space provided.

Prompt: Jamie got her first bank statement. She was looking it over and really trying to figure it out. Jamie would like you to help her reconcile her bank statement.

1. Explain to Jamie how to reconcile her bank statement.
2. Explain to Jamie why it is important to keep up with her bank account balance from one statement to the next.

Scoring Guide

- **4** Student gives correct answers for parts 1 and 2. All explanations are clear and complete. There is evidence of clear understanding of the concept.
- **3** Student gives correct answers for parts 1 and 2. Explanations are correct, but possibly unclear. There is less evidence of clear understanding.
- **2** Student answers 1 (1 or 2) part of the questions completely correct. There is some evidence of understanding.
- **1** Student gives only parts of correct answers. There is little evidence of understanding.
- **0** Response is totally incorrect or irrelevant (does not add any new information to the question).

Name: ______________________

Date: ______________________

Banking

OPEN RESPONSE #2

Please answer all parts of the question in the space provided.

Prompt: Daniel got a memo from the bank that one of the checks he had written was returned to the merchant. He now owed a $27 non-sufficient fund fee on his $32.89 purchase. He was not sure what was going to happen next.

The next day he received a telephone call from the merchant saying he owed $32.89 for the check plus a returned check fee of $25.

1. Explain to Daniel what happens when a bank notifies you of a non-sufficient fund on a check. How could he have prevented this from happening?
2. Calculate what Daniel's $32.89 purchase now cost him. Show or explain how you got your answer.

Scoring Guide

4 Student gives correct answers for parts 1 and 2. All explanations are clear and complete. There is evidence of clear understanding of the concept.

3 Student gives correct answers for parts 1 and 2. Explanations are correct, but possibly unclear. There is less evidence of clear understanding.

2 Student answers 1 (1 or 2) part of the questions completely correct. There is some evidence of understanding.

1 Student gives only parts of correct answers. There is little evidence of understanding.

0 Response is totally incorrect or irrelevant (does not add any new information to the question).

Savings

You can use the following math concepts in planning for your financial future. The first concept—**calculating interest earned on a deposit**—is useful to help you plan for the future. In most cases you will keep your emergency reserve funds in an interest-earning account. This calculation will help you determine how much money you expect to accumulate over the duration of the deposit.

The second concept—**calculating deposit interest with multiple compounding periods**—is a useful exercise to understand how increasing the frequency of compounding helps you grow wealth. Compounding is the process of adding the interest you have earned after some period of time back to the principal and then earning interest on that interest.

The third concept—**calculating annual percentage yield (APY)**—is useful because comparing APYs helps you determine which savings option will yield the best results over time. Sometimes a lower interest rate with higher compounding frequency will result in greater wealth accumulation. Comparing APYs allows you to immediately see which option is best.

The fourth concept—**calculating tax savings of retirement account contributions**—is useful because it will help you make timing decisions about contributions to tax-favored retirement accounts. Some accounts are tax deductible and reduce your current taxes. Others reduce your taxes at the time of withdrawal. The tax savings of different types of accounts may dictate which you decide to invest your money in.

Name: ____________________

Date: ____________________

CHAPTER 13

Savings

CONCEPT #1: Calculating Interest Earned on a Deposit

Savings accounts at a bank or credit union, money market accounts, and certificates of deposit (CDs) are just a few of the places where you can put money and earn interest. For this first concept, we'll look at how much interest you would earn over a period of time at different interest rates. For example, how much interest would you earn if you placed $1,000 in an interest-bearing account that paid an annual interest rate of 5 percent compounded annually? You would earn $1,000 × .05 = $50. Another way of looking at this question is to ask how much your deposit would be worth at the end of one year. To find the answer, you would simply multiply by $1,000 × (1 + .05) = $1,050. Multiplying by 1 gives you the original amount and multiplying by the .05 gives you the interest earned.

You will see that this formula is the same one used to calculate a future value:

$$\text{Future value} = \text{Present value}\ (1 + \text{interest rate})^{\text{number of periods}}$$

or

$$FV = PV(1 + i)^n$$
$$\text{So, } FV = \$1{,}000(1.05)^1 = \$1{,}050$$

Since the period in this example is only one year, n = 1. However, this formula will also work for multiple years as we will see in Concept #2 that follows.

Math Review

2,000 × .06 = ________ 3,000 × .07 = ________ 4,000 × .08 = ________

11,000 × .04 = ________ 28,500 × .035 = ________ 31,000 × .065 = ________

9,000 × 1.05 = ________ 13,000 × 1.07 = ________ 1,800 × 1.09 = ________

17,400 × 1.045 = ________ 7,200 × 1.0625 = ________ 9,150 × 1.055 = ________

MyFinLitLab **Apply Your Knowledge**

1. Judy put $2,000 in a CD earning 6 percent annually. How much interest will she earn over the year?

2. Phillip deposited $3,400 into a savings account that pays 4 percent annual interest. How much will he have in his account at the end of one year?

3. Tara bought a $5,000 CD that will pay 5.5 percent in annual interest. How much will the CD be worth at the end of the first year?

4. If Tara could get the same interest rate for the second year, how much would the CD be worth at the end of year two?

5. Landon has $8,400 in a savings account that pays 3 percent annual interest. How much interest will he earn on that account this year?

Name: ____________________

Date: ____________________

CHAPTER 13

Savings

CONCEPT #2: Calculating Deposit Interest with Multiple Compounding Periods

When you earn interest on savings, you have the opportunity to take advantage of compounding —earning interest on the interest you have earned. Compounding affects how much money you will accumulate over a multi-year period. For example, many CDs are two, three, four, or five years. Let's look at an example. Assume you deposited $5,000 in a CD that pays 5.5 percent annually. Assuming annual compounding, how much will you have accumulated after two years?

Remember the following formula:

$$\text{Future value} = \text{Present value}\ (1 + \text{interest rate})^{\text{number of periods}}$$

or

$$FV = PV(1 + i)^n$$

For this formula, the word *period* refers to the period of time at which compounding occurs. The number of periods is two for this problem, so you raise this figure to the second power.

$$\text{So, } FV = \$5{,}000(1.055)^2 = \$5{,}565.13$$

Now look back at Concept #1, Question 4. Did you get the same answer? You should have. How much interest did Tara earn over the two-year period? $5,565.13 – $5,000 = $565.13 in interest.

Math Review

$4{,}000(1.04)^2 =$ ______	$4{,}000(1.04)^3 =$ ______	$4{,}000(1.04)^4 =$ ______
$2{,}000(1.03)^2 =$ ______	$2{,}500(1.035)^2 =$ ______	$6{,}000(1.0425)^2 =$ ______
$1{,}800(1.01)^4 =$ ______	$15{,}000(1.06)^6 =$ ______	$1{,}000(1.01)^4 =$ ______
$3{,}200(1.02)^2 =$ ______	$3{,}200(1.02)^4 =$ ______	$3{,}200(1.01)^{12} =$ ______

MyFinLitLab **Apply Your Knowledge**

1. How much would you accumulate over a three-year period if you deposited $2,000 in an account earning 4 percent annually?

2. How much would you accumulate over a four-year period if you deposited $2,500 in an account earning 6 percent annually?

3. How much would you accumulate over a two-year period if you deposited $7,200 in an account earning 3 1/2 percent annually?

4. How much would you accumulate over a three-year period if you deposited $2,000 in an account earning 5 percent compounded annually?

5. How much would you accumulate over a six-year period if you deposited $3,000 in an account earning 8 percent annual interest that is compounded annually?

CHAPTER 13

Savings

CONCEPT #3: Calculating Annual Percentage Yield (APY)

In many savings vehicles, compounding occurs more often than every year. It is common, for example, for a bank to pay interest on a quarterly basis—that is, put a quarter of the year's interest in the account every three months. Then, that interest is in the account earning interest, so that the next quarter's earned interest is a little bit higher. With quarterly compounding, the account will actually earn more interest than the stated rate.

The annual percentage yield, or APY, is the annual rate of interest that factors in the effects of compounding. Savings institutions are required by law to provide you with APY information on their accounts so that you can make an accurate comparison between different savings accounts. APY allows you to compare apples with apples. APY is also known as the effective annual rate. The formula to calculate APY follows:

$$APY = \left[1 + \frac{i_{nom}}{m}\right]^m - 1$$

where

i_{nom} = the stated interest rate, or nominal interest rate

m = number of annual compounding periods; for example with quarterly compounding m = 4; semiannual compounding m = 2; monthly compounding m = 12; and so on.

As you can see, i_{nom} = period rate of interest; interest rate per quarter; interest rate per six month period; interest rate per month.

So, if you have a 5 percent rate of interest compounded quarterly you can calculate the APY.

$$APY = \left[1 + \frac{.05}{4}\right]^4 - 1 = 1.0125^4 - 1 = .05095 \text{ or } 5.095 \text{ percent.}$$

Math Review

$APY = \left[1 + \frac{.06}{2}\right]^2 - 1 =$ _______

$APY = \left[1 + \frac{.08}{2}\right]^2 - 1 =$ _______

$APY = \left[1 + \frac{.08}{4}\right]^4 - 1 =$ _______

$APY = \left[1 + \frac{.04}{4}\right]^4 - 1 =$ _______

$APY = \left[1 + \frac{.09}{12}\right]^{12} - 1 =$ _______

$APY = \left[1 + \frac{.12}{2}\right]^2 - 1 =$ _______

$APY = \left[1 + \frac{.03}{6}\right]^6 - 1 =$ _______

$APY = \left[1 + \frac{.12}{12}\right]^{12} - 1 =$ _______

MyFinLitLab **Apply Your Knowledge**

1. Kramer is thinking about buying a one-year CD with a 4 percent stated rate that compounds interest monthly. What is the APY of this CD?

2. Beyonce just deposited $2,000 cash into a savings account that has a stated rate of interest of 6 percent, but compounds the money quarterly. What is the APY of this option?

3. Refer to the previous question's answer. How much money will Beyonce have at the end of the year?

4. Moneica placed some money into a CD that pays 5 percent interest compounded semi-annually. What is the APY of this CD?

5. Carilla deposited $4,000 into a savings account earning 5.5 percent that is compounded monthly. What is the APY of this account?

Name: ____________________

Date: ____________________

CHAPTER 13

Savings

CONCEPT #4: Calculating Tax Savings of Retirement Account Contributions

There are various provisions within the IRS tax code that encourage some individuals to save money for retirement in certain types of accounts. In some cases, the contributions to these accounts reduce your immediate tax liability by allowing you to deduct this savings from your taxable income. For example, assume your taxable income was $40,000 and you opted to make a $1,000 contribution to a tax-deductible retirement account. This would reduce your taxable income to $39,000. You would no longer be required to pay federal taxes on that $1,000. If your marginal tax rate were 28 percent, this deduction would result in a federal tax savings of $280. Your tax liability would be that much less due to the reduction in taxable income. As you can see, the easiest way to calculate the value of the tax shield is to multiply the amount of the tax-deductible deposit by your marginal tax rate. The marginal tax rate is the tax rate that you would pay on the next dollar of taxable income. Since we have a progressive tax system—that is, tax rates are larger for higher levels of income—we also have different marginal tax rates depending on your level of income.

Math Review

4,000 × .28 = ______	1,200 × .15 = ______	2,000 × .33 = ______
3,000 × .28 = ______	2,200 × .15 = ______	4,000 × .33 = ______
2,400 × .28 = ______	3,100 × .15 = ______	2,700 × .33 = ______
1,900 × .28 = ______	1,850 × .15 = ______	3,250 × .33 = ______

MyFinLitLab **Apply Your Knowledge**

1. Gray made a $3,500 tax-deductible contribution to his individual retirement account (IRA). Assuming he is in a 28 percent tax bracket, how much will this contribution save him on his taxes?

2. Ramella put $2,000 into a tax-deductible retirement account. How much will she save on her tax bill if her marginal tax rate is 15 percent?

3. Karen contributed $2,300 to her IRA this year. How much will she save on her tax bill if her marginal tax rate is 33 percent?

4. Jason put $1,100 into his retirement savings account. Assuming he is in a 15 percent tax bracket, how much will he save on his tax bill?

5. Xavier is thinking about putting $3,000 into his IRA. Assuming he is in a 33 percent tax bracket, how much money will he save on his tax bill?

Name: ______________________

Date: ______________________

Savings

OPEN RESPONSE #1

Please answer all parts of the question in the space provided.

Prompt: Ashleigh wants to put away $1,000 so that it will begin to earn interest. She is unsure in which account to place her money. Her bank offers a two-year CD that pays an APY of 3.18 percent, a money market account that has an APY of 5.5 percent, and a savings account with an APY of 3.5 percent. Ashleigh will need to take out the money after high school graduation for her future studies. She has two years until graduation.

1. Explain to Ashleigh how to calculate the interest earned on her deposit with each account.

2. Calculate the interest earned on each deposit. Show and explain how you got your answer.

Scoring Guide

4 Student gives correct answers for parts 1 and 2. All explanations are clear and complete. There is evidence of clear understanding of the concept.

3 Student gives correct answers for parts 1 and 2. Explanations are correct, but possibly unclear. There is less evidence of clear understanding.

2 Student answers 1 (1 or 2) part of the questions completely correct. There is some evidence of understanding.

1 Student gives only parts of correct answers. There is little evidence of understanding.

0 Response is totally incorrect or irrelevant (does not add any new information to the question).

Name: ____________________

Date: ____________________

Savings

OPEN RESPONSE #2

Please answer all parts of the question in the space provided.

Prompt: Josiah has just begun his first full-time job. He is trying to figure out how much money he should put in the company retirement account. Josiah's income is $35,000. This will put him in the marginal tax rate of 28 percent. He is trying to decide if he should contribute $1,500 or $2,500 to the company's tax-deductible retirement account.

1. Explain to Josiah why it is good to contribute to a tax-deductible retirement account.
2. Calculate what Josiah's tax savings would be for each amount he is considering to contribute to his company's tax-deductible retirement account. Show and explain how you got your answer.

Scoring Guide

4 Student gives correct answers for parts 1 and 2. All explanations are clear and complete. There is evidence of clear understanding of the concept.

3 Student gives correct answers for parts 1 and 2. Explanations are correct, but possibly unclear. There is less evidence of clear understanding.

2 Student answers 1 (1 or 2) part of the questions completely correct. There is some evidence of understanding.

1 Student gives only parts of correct answers. There is little evidence of understanding.

0 Response is totally incorrect or irrelevant (does not add any new information to the question).

Investing

You can use the following math concepts in planning for your financial future. The first concept—**calculating holding period returns**—is useful because it allows you to determine the size of your gain or loss in percentage terms over the life of your investment. You can use this concept for any type of investment, such as houses, cars, stocks, bonds, mutual funds, and others.

The second concept—**calculating dollar returns on a stock**—is a useful exercise because you will need this information for tax purposes. If you sell a stock during the tax year you will have to determine your gain or loss and will either pay taxes on the gain or potentially receive a tax benefit from the loss.

The third concept—**calculating a rate of return on stocks**—helps you make investment decisions about buying or selling stocks. Remember, we buy stocks to make money, and you want your percentage return to be greater than the amount you could earn in lower risk or risk-free investments. If you can make more money in a bank CD, then you don't need to assume the higher risk associated with owning stocks.

The fourth concept—**calculating a rate of return on bonds**—helps you make investment decisions. For example, you might calculate a percentage return using today's market value of a bond and decide to sell it based on that information. You may also use this calculation and determine you would like to buy a specific bond based on your forecasts.

Name: ____________________

Date: ____________________

CHAPTER 14

Investing

CONCEPT #1: Calculating Holding Period Returns

In your financial life, there will be a number of situations in which you will want to know what your percentage return is over the period of time you have held some asset. For example, maybe you paid $45,000 for some land four years ago and and you recently sold that same property for $62,000. What was your holding period return (HPR)? You will use the following formula to calculate this return.

$$HPR = (P_1 - P_0) \div P_0$$

Notice that this is the same formula we used in Chapter 8 to calculate a rate of change. So our HPR = ($62,000 – $45,000) ÷ $45,000 = .37778, or 37.78 percent return over the four-year period. Be careful not to compare one holding period return to another unless the holding periods are the same length, or it is a meaningless comparison. Also note that holding period returns can be negative.

Math Review

(12,000 – 9,900) ÷ 9,900 = ________

(313,000 – 299,500) ÷ 299,500 = ________

(2,120 – 1,900) ÷ 1,900 = ________

(25,100 – 28,300) ÷ 28,300 = ________

(34,000 – 29,500) ÷ 29,500 = ________

(71,000 – 59,200) ÷ 59,200 = ________

(22,400 – 18,140) ÷ 18,140 = ________

(11,125 – 12,550) ÷ 12,550 = ________

MyFinLitLab **Apply Your Knowledge**

1. Lakita bought a painting from an up-and-coming artist for $550. She sold it three years later for $875. What was her holding period return?

2. Clay paid $22,000 for a building lot in a subdivision with the intent to build a house later. However, he got a promotion that required him to move, and he only was able to sell the lot two years later for $19,500. What was his holding period return?

3. Zak bought a car from a newspaper ad for $4,100. He put another $1,000 in a paint job and sold the car two months later for $6,700. What was his holding period return?

4. Karissa bought a small house to use as a rental for $87,000. However, someone immediately offered her $95,000 for the house. What was her holding period return?

5. Devon paid $1,200 for a baseball card collection. She turned around and sold the cards individually on eBay for $1,745 in total. What was her holding period return?

Name: ____________________

Date: ____________________

Investing

CONCEPT #2: Calculating Dollar Returns on a Stock

When you start investing, you will find that as you buy and sell financial assets like stocks or bonds, you will need to calculate dollar returns for tax purposes. You also will want to monitor the success of your investment strategy. In some cases you will make money and have a gain. In other cases you will lose money and have a loss. In the case of stocks, you can make money by selling the stock for more than you paid for it and you also may receive dividends while you own the stock. For example, assume you bought 100 shares of stock in XYZ company for $23 a share and sold it one year later for $31.50 a share. You also received a $2 dividend during the time you owned the stock. What was your dollar return?

$$100(\$31.50 - \$23) + 100(\$2) = \$1{,}050$$

Remember: When you compare dollar returns of different investments, you must factor in the amount of time you have held the investments. A $500 return in one year may be more impressive than a $900 return in two.

Math Review

100(52.15 – 48.25) = _______

150(23.45 – 19.75) + 150(4) = _______

110(23.50 – 19.13) = _______

225(51.50 – 39.50) + 225(1.25) = _______

50(113.00 – 110.25) = _______

20(38.25 – 39.75) + 20(1) = _______

300(85.43 – 98.25) = _______

72(11.25 – 10.75) + 72(2.10) = _______

MyFinLitLab Apply Your Knowledge

1. Sharon just sold 50 shares of stock for $32.50 a share. What was her dollar return on this stock if she paid $24.88 a share for it when she bought it?

2. Carmen bought 115 shares of stock for $45.75 a share. She collected two dividend payments of $2 per share each year and later sold the stock for $51.38 a share. What was her dollar return on this stock?

3. Darius bought 100 shares of stock for $57.25 a share. He sold it one year later for $55 a share. He also collected $4 a share in dividends over the time he held the stock. What was his dollar return on this investment?

4. Syed bought 40 shares of stock for $42 a share that he later sold for $38 a share. What was his dollar return on this investment?

5. Lindley paid $67 a share for 175 shares of stock in a company that she later sold for $87 a share. What was her dollar return on this stock?

Name: ____________________

Date: ____________________

Investing

CONCEPT #3: Calculating a Rate of Return on Stocks

Calculating a percentage return on your investments helps you make comparisons when you are looking at how investments of different dollar amounts have performed. This process can be useful to determine if one investment strategy is outperforming another.

Remember: Stocks have two possible cash inflows: 1) dividends and 2) proceeds from sale of the stock. We will use the same holding period return formula we used earlier. Let's look at an example. Assume you bought a stock for $45 a share and sold it later for $47.50 a share. You also received a dividend distribution of $2 a share while you owned the stock. What was your rate of return on this investment?

$$\text{HPR} = (P_1 - P_0) \div P_0$$

(($47.50 – $45) + $2) ÷ $45 = .10 ,or 10 percent. Note that the numerator will contain the dividend and the gain or loss on the stock transaction.

Math Review

((56 – 52.50) + 1.40) ÷ 52.50 = ________

((74.25 – 69.75) + 3) ÷ 69.75 = ________

((26.50 – 22.20) + 2.10) ÷ 22.20 = ________

((11.50 – 9.75) + 1) ÷ 9.75 = ________

((44 – 43.50) + .50) ÷ 43.50 = ________

((53.25 – 59.50) + 2.25) ÷ 59.50 = ________

((61.25 – 62.50) + 1.55) ÷ 62.50 = ________

((31.50 – 28.75) + 2.75) ÷ 28.75 = ________

MyFinLitLab **Apply Your Knowledge**

1. Jessica sold stock for $52 a share that she bought for $48.50 a share. She also received a $1.10 dividend while she owned the stock. What was her rate of return on her investment?

2. Camerosa bought stock for $23 a share and later sold it for $27. What was her rate of return?

3. Roland sold some stock for $89.25 a share that he paid $99 a share for. He also collected a $3 dividend while he owned the stock. What was his rate of return?

4. Yola bought stock for $32.50 a share and later sold it for $38 a share. The stock did not pay dividends. What was her rate of return?

5. Nika bought stock in a company for $56 a share. She later sold it for $58 a share but she also collected a $4 dividend while she held the stock. What was her rate of return?

Name: ______________________

Date: ______________________

CHAPTER 14

Investing

CONCEPT #4: Calculating a Rate of Return on Bonds

Just as with stock returns, you may want to compare bond strategies. Or you may want to compare your bond returns with the returns of your other investments, such as stock or real estate. Calculating a percentage return on bonds will allow you to make these comparisons when you are using the same time horizon. Obviously it does not make sense to compare a two-year percentage return to a one-year percentage return.

Let's look at a bond example. Bonds have two possible sources of income: 1) Most bonds make interest payments to the bondholders and 2) you may sell a bond for more than you paid for it. What is the rate of return on a bond that you sold for $1,100 if you paid $1,050 for and you also collected $80 in interest over the time you held the bond?

The holding period return (HPR) formula we used earlier works on bonds as well.

$$HPR = (P_1 - P_0) \div P_0$$

So, (($1,100 – $1,050) + $80) ÷ $1,050 = .12381 or 12.38 percent. Note that in the numerator we now have our gain or loss on the bond plus our interest received.

Math Review

((1,023 – 922.50) + 100) ÷ 922.50 = ________

((893.25 – 926.75) + 80) ÷ 926.75 = ________

((998.25 – 936.50) + 120) ÷ 936.50 = ________

((1,144.25 – 1,015.75) + 90) ÷ 1,015.75 = ________

((1,006.50 – 987.25) + 200) ÷ 987.25 = ________

((996.25 – 1,121.75) + 100) ÷ 1,121.75 = ________

MyFinLitLab Apply Your Knowledge

1. Camilla sold a bond for $1,100 that she bought for $1,009.50. She also collected $45 in interest while she held the bond. What was her rate of return?

2. What is the rate of return on a bond you bought for $897.25 and later sold for $910 if you also collected $120 in interest while you owned that bond?

3. Leon paid $855.25 for a bond that he later sold for $984. He did not collect any interest while he owned the bond. What was his rate of return?

4. Gladys bought a bond for $928.50 and later sold it for 1,008.25. She also collected $50 in interest while she owned the bond. What was her rate of return?

5. Kelsey paid $1,198 for a bond that she later sold for $1,111. She collected $60 in interest while she owned the bond. What was her rate of return?

Name: ____________________

Date: ____________________

CHAPTER 14

Investing

OPEN RESPONSE #1

Please answer all parts of the question in the space provided.

Prompt: Maxsim's grandfather purchased four acres of land as a present for Maxsim's sixteenth birthday. The purchase cost $8,000 five years ago. Now Maxsim is about to graduate from college and is thinking of selling the property. The property is now worth $35,000.

1. Explain to Maxsim how to calculate his holding period return. Why might he want to hold onto or sell this property? What risk will he take if he decides to hold on or sell?

2. Calculate Maxsim's holding period return at this time. Show and explain how you got your answer.

Scoring Guide

4 Student gives correct answers for parts 1 and 2. All explanations are clear and complete. There is evidence of clear understanding of the concept.

3 Student gives correct answers for parts 1 and 2. Explanations are correct, but possibly unclear. There is less evidence of clear understanding.

2 Student answers 1 (1 or 2) part of the questions completely correct. There is some evidence of understanding.

1 Student gives only parts of correct answers. There is little evidence of understanding.

0 Response is totally incorrect or irrelevant (does not add any new information to the question).

Name: ______________________

Date: ______________________

CHAPTER 14

Investing

OPEN RESPONSE #2

Please answer all parts of the question in the space provided.

Prompt: Karina is wondering about stocks and bonds that were purchased in her name at her birth. With the volatile market, she wants to calculate her rate of return on each at this time to determine if she needs to sell or stay with each.

She has one bond that was purchased for $1,000 on which she has collected $900 in interest over the past 18 years. The bond is now worth $1,050. She also owns 100 shares of stock that was initially bought for $10 and would sell at this time for $10.50. She has received a total of $8 a share in dividend distributions while owning the stock.

1. Explain to Karina the two possible sources of income for bonds and the two sources of cash inflows for stocks.

2. Calculate Karina's rate of return for the stock and the bond. Show and explain how you got your answer.

Scoring Guide

4 Student gives correct answers for parts 1 and 2. All explanations are clear and complete. There is evidence of clear understanding of the concept.

3 Student gives correct answers for parts 1 and 2. Explanations are correct, but possibly unclear. There is less evidence of clear understanding.

2 Student answers 1 (1 or 2) part of the questions completely correct. There is some evidence of understanding.

1 Student gives only parts of correct answers. There is little evidence of understanding.

0 Response is totally incorrect or irrelevant (does not add any new information to the question).

Time Value of Money

You can use the following math concepts in planning for your financial future. The first concept—**calculating simple interest**—is useful for determining interest on certain deposit accounts. The concept of simple interest also provides an important contrast to compound interest and highlights the importance of compounding.

The second concept—**calculating future value with compound interest**—is useful because it helps you to understand the importance of putting your money to work for you. When you begin to earn interest on your interest (compounding), you will start to grow wealth quickly. Future value calculations also allow you to determine how much money to save today in order to achieve your desired financial goals at some later date.

The third concept—**calculating present value**—is a useful exercise to understand certain investments. One way to evaluate investment options is to forecast the cash flows you expect to earn from those investments and to convert them into a present value. The process of calculating the present value of cash flows is commonly called discounting and the interest rate used to calculate the present value is commonly called the discount rate.

The fourth concept—**calculating the present value of an annuity**—is similar to calculating present values of a single sum, only now you are incorporating a stream of equal cash flows. Rental income would be one example of an equal income stream occurring at equal intervals (annuity).

The fifth concept—**calculating the future value of an annuity**—is useful because it enables you to determine how much money to save or invest every month to achieve a future financial objective or goal. What if you wanted to accumulate $1 million by the time you were 50? This tool will help you determine how much to save every month to achieve that objective.

The sixth concept—**calculating payment amounts**—is useful any time you are interested in buying an asset over time. Houses, cars, boats, land, and furniture are all examples of assets you may finance. With this concept, you can calculate your payment before you begin shopping. How much can you afford? This tool will help you make better decisions about the payment amounts of expected purchases before you shop.

***Note*: Some of your answers may differ slightly due to rounding errors. Your results will depend on how many decimal places you use for these calculations.**

Name: ____________________

Date: ____________________

CHAPTER 15

Time Value of Money

CONCEPT #1: Calculating Simple Interest

Simple interest is what you earn when you only earn interest on the principal invested. In fact, most investments or savings you make in real life will feature some kind of compounding—in which interest is periodically added to the account, where it compounds, or earns interest on itself. However, calculating simple interest is a useful exercise for comparison purposes and an easy way to understand the concept of interest. Interest is essentially rent paid on money borrowed or rent received on money loaned. Simple interest is calculated by the following:

Dollar amount of interest = principal × interest rate × time period

For example, how much simple interest would you earn on a $2,000 two-year deposit that was 5 percent simple interest?

$2,000 × .05 × 2 = $200

Math Review

3,500 × .06 × 3 = ________

4,100 × .07 × 1 = ________

5,000 × .04 × 3 = ________

500 × .08 × 4 = ________

2,500 × .09 × 2 = ________

7,000 × .045 × 2 = ________

4,500 × .055 × 5 = ________

1,200 × .09 × 2.5 = ________

3,000 × .02 × 6 = ________

5,300 × .05 × 3 = ________

2,800 × .035 × 3 = ________

4,600 × .05 × 4 = ________

MyFinLitLab **Apply Your Knowledge**

1. Benjamin deposited $4,000 into an account earning 5 percent simple interest for one year. How much interest will he earn during the year?

2. Deidra put $2,350 into an account that pays 6 percent simple interest. How much money will she have after two years if she leaves the money in her account?

3. Heath put $2,000 into an account earning 7 percent simple interest. How much interest will he earn over a three-year period?

4. Kim deposited $3,200 into an account earning 8 percent simple interest for 18 months. How much interest will she earn over that period?

5. Faisal has $7,000 that he will deposit into an account earning 6.5 percent simple interest for 3.5 years. How much interest will he earn on this account?

Name: ____________

Date: ____________

Time Value of Money

CONCEPT #2: Calculating Future Value with Compound Interest

Compound interest is such a powerful financial tool for wealth accumulation that it has been dubbed "the miracle of compound interest." With time on your side, you can use the power of compounding to turn small sums into large sums. And, the higher the return you earn on your investment, the larger the end result.

The formula for future value with compounding as follows:

$$FV = PV(1 + i)^n$$

where

FV = future value
PV = present value or the amount you initially invest
i = interest rate
n = number of compounding periods

Let's look at an example. Assume you invest \$2,000 for 20 years at an interest rate of 8 percent. How much would your initial \$2,000 investment grow to over that time period?

$$FV = \$2,000(1 + .08)^{20} = \$9,321.91$$

Math Review

$\$2,500(1 + .05)^{25}$ = ________

$\$6,000(1 + .06)^{30}$ = ________

$\$4,000(1 + .12)^{22}$ = ________

$\$5,000(1 + .075)^{27}$ = ________

$\$11,000(1 + .04)^{40}$ = ________

$\$2,000(1 + .12)^{25}$ = ________

$\$2,000(1 + .18)^{40}$ = ________

$\$9,000(1 + .08)^{40}$ = ________

MyFinLitLab **Apply Your Knowledge**

1. How much could you accumulate over a 30-year period if you deposited \$3,500 in an account earning 9 percent compounded annually?

2. How much could you accumulate over a 40-year period if you deposited \$3,500 in an account earning 9 percent compounded annually?

3. How much could you accumulate over a 50-year period if you deposited \$3,500 in an account earning 9 percent compounded annually?

4. How much could you accumulate over a 30-year period if you deposited $3,500 in an account earning 12 percent compounded annually?

5. How much could you accumulate over a 40-year period if you deposited $3,500 in an account earning 12 percent compounded annually?

6. How much could you accumulate over a 50-year period if you deposited $3,500 in an account earning 12 percent compounded annually?

Now maybe you can begin to understand why it is called the "miracle of compound interest." If you deposited $3,500 at age 18 and could earn a 12 percent annual return you could accumulate over $1,000,000 by the time you turn 68.

Name: ______________________

Date: ______________________

Time Value of Money

CONCEPT #3: Calculating Present Value

Present-value calculations involve taking some value that you will receive in the future and then calculating an equivalent amount in today's dollars. Given the option, all of us would prefer to have some amount of money in our hands today instead of one or two years from now. That's because we could deposit that money and begin to earn interest on it now. That means there is an opportunity cost associated with waiting a couple of years for the money—the cost of the interest earned during that interval. Present-value calculations consider that opportunity cost and equate that lump sum amount in the future to the equivalent amount today.

For example, assume you have been promised $1,000 when you graduate in one year, but that you could earn a return of 5 percent annually on that money if you had it today. The present value of that future $1,000 can be calculated with the following formula:

$$PV = FV \div (1 + i)^n$$

where

FV = future value

PV = present value or the amount you initially invest

i = interest rate

n = number of compounding periods

Let's look at our example:

$$PV = \$1,000 \div (1 + .05)^1 = \$952.38$$

In other words, we could accept $952.38 today and invest it at 5 percent and we would have that same $1,000 at the end of the year. You can check your answer by computing the future value using the formula from Concept #2.

$$FV = \$952.38(1 + .05) = \$1,000$$

Math Review

$\$2,000 \div (1 + .03)^2 =$ ________

$\$5,000 \div (1 + .05)^3 =$ ________

$\$7,500 \div (1 + .08)^7 =$ ________

$\$4,000 \div (1 + .06)^3 =$ ________

$\$11,000 \div (1 + .15)^5 =$ ________

$\$15,000 \div (1 + .105)^4 =$ ________

$\$1,500 \div (1 + .02)^7 =$ ________

$\$21,000 \div (1 + .11)^9 =$ ________

MyFinLitLab **Apply Your Knowledge**

1. What is the present value of $5,000 you will receive in four years given an interest rate of 6 percent?

2. What is the present value of $23,000 you will receive in six years given an interest rate of 5 percent?

3. What is the present value of $105,000 you will receive in 11 years given an interest rate of 4.5 percent?

4. What is the present value of $8,200 you will receive in two years given an interest rate of 7 percent?

5. What is the present value of $50,000 you will receive in seven years given an interest rate of 9 percent?

Name: ____________________

Date: ____________________

CHAPTER 15

Time Value of Money

CONCEPT #4: Calculating Present Value of an Annuity

Calculating the present value of an annuity is useful for determining the value of any equal cash flow occurring at equal intervals using some given interest rate. It is conceptually the same as Concept #3, except now we are working with multiple equal cash flows. For example, maybe you sold a car on credit to a friend for $1,200 a year for two years. Assuming you could earn 5 percent interest on your money, what single amount today is equivalent to receiving two annual payments of $1,200 each?

The formula for the present value of an annuity follows:

$$\text{PVann} = \text{PMT(PVIFA)}$$

Since, $\text{PVIFA} = \left[\left(\frac{1}{i}\right) - \left(\frac{1}{i(1+i)^n}\right)\right]$, then $\text{PVann} = \text{PMT}\left[\left(\frac{1}{i}\right) - \left(\frac{1}{i(1+i)^n}\right)\right]$.

So in this case, $\text{PVann} = \$1,200\left[\left(\frac{1}{.05}\right) - \left(\frac{1}{.05(1.05)^2}\right)\right] = \$2,233.27$.

Math Review

$\$2,000\left[\left(\frac{1}{.08}\right) - \left(\frac{1}{.08(1.08)^{10}}\right)\right] =$ ________

$\$500\left[\left(\frac{1}{.095}\right) - \left(\frac{1}{.095(1.095)^{12}}\right)\right] =$ ________

$\$3,200\left[\left(\frac{1}{.12}\right) - \left(\frac{1}{.12(1.12)^{7}}\right)\right] =$ ________

$\$10,000\left[\left(\frac{1}{.04}\right) - \left(\frac{1}{.04(1.04)^{25}}\right)\right] =$ ________

$\$5,000\left[\left(\frac{1}{.06}\right) - \left(\frac{1}{.06(1.06)^{8}}\right)\right] =$ ________

$\$1,500\left[\left(\frac{1}{.07}\right) - \left(\frac{1}{.07(1.07)^{9}}\right)\right] =$ ________

MyFinLitLab **Apply Your Knowledge**

1. What is the present value of $2,400 a year for 15 years given a discount rate (interest rate) of 5 percent?

2. What is the present value of $4,000 a year for 10 years given a discount rate (interest rate) of 7 percent?

3. What is the present value of $5,000 a year for 20 years given a discount rate (interest rate) of 8 percent?

4. What is the present value of $1,400 a year for 5 years given a discount rate (interest rate) of 2 percent?

5. What is the present value of $25,000 a year for 30 years given a discount rate (interest rate) of 6 percent?

Name: ____________________

Date: ____________________

CHAPTER 15

Time Value of Money

CONCEPT #5: Calculating Future Value of an Annuity

Calculating the future value of an annuity helps you determine how much you can accumulate over time given a regular savings pattern. For example, maybe you want to know how much money you can accumulate over a 30-year period if you invest $2,000 a year and can earn 10 percent annually. The formula for this calculation follows:

$$FVann = PMT(FVIFA)$$

Since, $FVIFA = \left[\frac{(1+i)^n - 1}{i}\right]$, then $FVann = PMT\left[\frac{(1+i)^n - 1}{i}\right]$.

So in this case, $FVann = \$2,000\left[\frac{(1+.10)^{30} - 1}{.10}\right] = \$2,000(164.494) = \$328,988.05$.

Math Review

$\$3,000\left[\frac{(1+.12)^{40} - 1}{.12}\right] =$ ____________________

$\$2,400\left[\frac{(1+.08)^{30} - 1}{.08}\right] =$ ____________________

$\$4,000\left[\frac{(1+.09)^{25} - 1}{.09}\right] =$ ____________________

$\$12,000\left[\frac{(1+.10)^{40} - 1}{.10}\right] =$ ____________________

$\$1,000\left[\frac{(1+.07)^{50} - 1}{.07}\right] =$ ____________________

$\$4,800\left[\frac{(1+.09)^{40} - 1}{.09}\right] =$ ____________________

MyFinLitLab **Apply Your Knowledge**

1. How much money could you accumulate if you invested $3,600 a year for 25 years and could earn 8 percent interest?

2. How much money could you accumulate if you invested $6,000 a year for 35 years and could earn 10 percent interest?

3. How much money could you accumulate if you invested $2,400 a year for 50 years and could earn 9 percent interest?

4. How much money could you accumulate if you invested $1,800 a year for 45 years and could earn 12 percent interest?

5. How much money could you accumulate if you invested $800 a year for 50 years and could earn 7 percent interest?

Name: ____________________

Date: ____________________

CHAPTER 15

Time Value of Money

CONCEPT #6: Calculating Payments

This concept is extremely useful when you want to know how much your payments would be on any major purchase that you finance. People typically finance houses, cars, boats, land, and other assets. In most cases you will calculate monthly payments.

Remember from Concept #4 that PVann = PMT(PVIFA). We can use this same formula and solve for PMT as follows:

$$\text{PMT} = \text{PVann} \div \text{PVIFA}$$

And, when we are solving for payment amount (PMT) we actually know the PVann: it's the amount we are financing. For example, if a house is selling for $100,000, that is the present value, or PVann, in our formula. So our house PMT would be PMT = $100,000 ÷ PVIFA. And you calculate the PVIFA using the exact same formula we used in Concept #4 as follows:

$$\text{PVIFA} = \left[\left(\frac{1}{i}\right) - \left(\frac{1}{i(1+i)^n}\right)\right]$$

So, PMT = $ amount financed $\div \left[\left(\frac{1}{i}\right) - \left(\frac{1}{i(1+i)^n}\right)\right]$.

If you are looking for monthly payments, you simply convert the interest rate (i) to a monthly rate by dividing by 12 and convert the number of annual periods to monthly periods by multiplying by 12. For example, $100,000 financed over a five-year period at an annual interest rate of 6 percent would have n = 5 × 12 = 60 and i = .06 ÷ 12 = .005.

$$\text{So, PMT} = \$100{,}000 \div \left[\left(\frac{1}{.005}\right) - \left(\frac{1}{.005(1.005)^{60}}\right)\right] = \$100{,}000 \div 51.63205 = \$1{,}936.78 \text{ per month.}$$

Math Review

$$\text{PMT} = \$24{,}000 \div \left[\left(\frac{1}{.005}\right) - \left(\frac{1}{.005(1.005)^{72}}\right)\right] = \underline{\hspace{6cm}}$$

$$\text{PMT} = \$200{,}000 \div \left[\left(\frac{1}{.01}\right) - \left(\frac{1}{.01(1.01)^{360}}\right)\right] = \underline{\hspace{6cm}}$$

$$\text{PMT} = \$150{,}000 \div \left[\left(\frac{1}{.0067}\right) - \left(\frac{1}{.0067(1.0067)^{180}}\right)\right] = \underline{\hspace{6cm}}$$

$$PMT = \$10,000 \div \left[\left(\frac{1}{.0075}\right) - \left(\frac{1}{.0075(1.0075)^{36}}\right)\right] = \underline{\hspace{6cm}}$$

MyFinLitLab **Apply Your Knowledge**

1. Calculate the monthly payment on a house you are thinking about purchasing. The loan amount will be $145,000 and will be financed at a 6 percent rate for 30 years.

2. Calculate the monthly payment on a car you are buying. You intend to finance $7,500 for 30 months at an 8 percent annual interest rate.

3. Calculate the monthly payment of some farm land you are considering buying. The amount you finance will be $225,000 at 4 percent for 40 years.

4. Calculate the monthly payment on a new car that will cost you $16,500. You intend to finance the entire amount over a five-year period at 3.9 percent annual interest.

5. Toyota is advertising 0 percent financing for 36 months on selected models. How much would the monthly payment be on a $22,000 car with this option?

Name: ______________________

Date: ______________________

Time Value of Money

OPEN RESPONSE #1

Please answer all parts of the question in the space provided.

Prompt: Derek wants to deposit $1,500. He has looked at two different accounts. One account will earn interest of 8 percent only on the principle. In another account the interest will compound over time at 8 percent.

1. Explain to Derek the difference in simple interest and compound interest.
2. Calculate Derek's earnings for two years for each of the accounts. Show and explain how you got your answer.

Scoring Guide

4 Student gives correct answers for parts 1 and 2. All explanations are clear and complete. There is evidence of clear understanding of the concept.

3 Student gives correct answers for parts 1 and 2. Explanations are correct, but possibly unclear. There is less evidence of clear understanding.

2 Student answers 1 (1 or 2) part of the questions completely correct. There is some evidence of understanding.

1 Student gives only parts of correct answers. There is little evidence of understanding.

0 Response is totally incorrect or irrelevant (does not add any new information to the question).

Name: ____________________

Date: ____________________

Time Value of Money

OPEN RESPONSE #2

Please answer all parts of the question in the space provided.

Prompt: Zoe's parents have rental property that they want to give to Zoe when she turns 21. The property brings in $1,600 a month, and her parents put this money in an account that earns 6 percent annually. Zoe wants to calculate the future value of this investment over the next four years until her 21st birthday.

1. Explain to Zoe how to calculate future value of an annuity.
2. Calculate the future value of Zoe's annuity on her 21st birthday. Show and explain how you got your answer.

Scoring Guide

4 Student gives correct answers for parts 1 and 2. All explanations are clear and complete. There is evidence of clear understanding of the concept.

3 Student gives correct answers for parts 1 and 2. Explanations are correct, but possibly unclear. There is less evidence of clear understanding.

2 Student answers 1 (1 or 2) part of the questions completely correct. There is some evidence of understanding.

1 Student gives only parts of correct answers. There is little evidence of understanding.

0 Response is totally incorrect or irrelevant (does not add any new information to the question).

Miscellaneous Financial Calculations

You can use the following math concepts in planning for your financial future. The first concept—**calculating a sale price**—is useful for shopping. Many people like to buy items on sale. Sales are often expressed in terms such as *half price,* or *30 percent off*. How much will you really pay for the item?

The second concept—**making foreign currency exchanges**—is a useful exercise for understanding how much something costs when priced in a foreign currency. You can use this when you travel abroad, but also when buying products on the Internet. With the Internet, you may purchase goods from another country and have them shipped to your door. In most cases, they will not be priced in U.S. dollars. So, how much will something really cost you?

The third concept—**calculating miles per gallon**—is useful because it will help you in planning for long trips. How much will it cost to go on spring break to the beach if you are going to drive? How about trips back and forth from home to college? You will find many times when you need to calculate your fuel efficiency and to use that information for planning.

The fourth concept—**calculating tips**—is useful when you dine out. In most restaurants, a tip is expected for good service. How large does the tip need to be? In general, tips are expressed as a percent of the cost of the meal. This exercise will help you understand how to make that calculation.

Name: ____________________

Date: ____________________

CHAPTER 16

Miscellaneous Financial Calculations

CONCEPT #1: Calculating a Sales Price

Retail stores often uses store "sales" to attract more buyers. Sometimes you may find it useful to calculate what the final price of an item will be after deducting the sales discount. For example, you may see coats advertised at "40 percent off sticker price" or tag price. In such a case, how much would a coat with a tag price of $120 cost you? You can calculate the final price by multiplying the tag price × (1 – percentage off). So the price in this case is $120 × (1 – .40) = $120 × .60 = $72.

Math Review

200(1 – .30) = ________	400 × (1 – .25) = ________	500(1 – .50) = ________
250(1 – .35) = ________	105 × (1 – 45) = ________	120(1 – .20) = ________
110(1 – .40) = ________	620 × (1 – .65) = ________	80(1 – .70) = ________
50(1 – .80) = ________	1,100 × (1 – .30) = ________	58(1 – .40) = ________

MyFinLitLab **Apply Your Knowledge**

1. Jillian saw a winter coat on sale in the spring. The coat was originally priced at $550, but had a "75 percent off" sign above the rack. How much will this coat cost?

2. Laura saw a furniture store sale that advertised "½ off." How much would a $2,400 living room suite cost on sale?

3. Keidra found several blouses on sale for 65 percent off. How much would a blouse priced at $45 cost on sale?

4. Jomé found a guitar on sale after the holidays for 40 percent off. If the guitar was normally $1,500 how much will it cost now?

5. Kalli wanted to buy a new dress for prom but it was priced at $875. The woman at the store whispered to her that it would be on sale next week for 30 percent off. How much will it cost then?

Name: ____________________

Date: ____________________

Miscellaneous Financial Calculations

CONCEPT #2: Making Foreign Currency Exchanges

At some point you will need to make foreign currency conversions. You will either travel abroad or purchase something in another currency on the Internet. Common currencies that you may ultimately need to exchange include Euros, Mexican pesos, Canadian dollars, British pounds, and Japanese yen. The same concept will apply to all conversions, but for now we will focus on the converting Euros to U.S. dollars and also converting Japanese yen to U.S. dollars. These currencies will have a conversion rate that varies depending on market conditions. For this exercise, use the following conversion rates:

EUR/USD 1.2827 or €1 = $1.2827

USD/JPY 96.35 or $1 = ¥96.35

These quotes are at a point in time and are called spot rates. Five minutes later the rates can be different, although there will likely be little change. Note that these quotes represent two different ways of quoting a currency. One rate is quoted in the dollar price of the currency. For example, one euro will cost a little more than $1.28 U.S. This type of quote where the foreign currency is stated in the home currency's price is known as a direct quote. The second quotation tells us we can buy 96.35 Japanese yen for every $1. This type of currency quote is known as an indirect quote. Note that a direct quote is the inverse of an indirect quote. For example, we can obtain an indirect quote of euros by taking €1 ÷ $1.2827 = .7796. This means that every U.S. dollar is worth .7796 euros. We can also convert the indirect quote on Japanese yen into a direct quote by $1 ÷ 96.35 yen = .01038. Each yen is equal to 1.038 cents, or a little more than a penny.

Using the exchange rates given above convert something priced at 40 euros into U.S. dollars. You simply multiply 40 × $1.2827 = $51.31. You can obtain the same result by dividing 40 by .7796.

Math Review

50 × 1.2827 = ________

96,000 ÷ 96.35 = ________

22 × 1.2827 = ________

650 × 1.2827 = ________

5,000 ÷ 96.35 = ________

101 × 1.2827 = ________

72 × 1.4127 = ________

8,250 ÷ 105.51 = ________

41 × 1.5238 = ________

17,090 ÷ 102.84 = ________

77,000 ÷ 96.35 = ________

89 × 1.2827 = ________

MyFinLitLab **Apply Your Knowledge**

1. Sherril is planning a trip to Europe this spring. Her hotel rate is quoted at €200 a night. How much is that in U.S. dollars given an exchange rate of €1 = $1.3271?

2. Jamison bought something on eBay priced at ¥92,500. How much did it cost him in U.S. dollars assuming an exchange rate of $1 = ¥106.56?

3. Gaile is planning a trip to France and has saved $700 for spending money. How many euros will that convert to at an exchange rate of €1 = $1.4124?

4. Burris wants to go to Japan for a semester. He has found an apartment in Tokyo that will cost ¥120,000 a month. How much is that in U.S. dollars assuming an exchange rate of $1 = ¥134.11?

5. Randolph wants to buy a gift in Germany this summer that will cost €55. He expects the exchange rate to be about €1 = $1.25. How much will the gift cost in U.S. dollars?

Name: ____________________

Date: ____________________

Miscellaneous Financial Calculations

CONCEPT #3: Calculating Miles per Gallon (MPG)

For vacation planning and budgeting in general, it is often useful to be able to calculate our fuel efficiency or the average miles we can drive per gallon of gasoline (MPG). For example owe may be planning a trip of 1,000 miles this summer for vacation. How much should we budget for gasoline if we think gas will be $2 a gallon or cheaper? That depends on the fuel efficiency, or MPG, of your vehicle. To determine your MPG, you fill up your tank with gas and record your vehicle's mileage. Later, when your tank is nearing empty, you fill up again and note the number of gallons required to refill your tank. Then you simply divide the number of miles you drove on that tank of gas by the number of gallons required to refill the tank. For example, assume you drove 368 miles on a tank of gas, and it took 15.8 gallons to refill your tank. Your MPG is therefore 368 miles ÷ 15.8 gallons = 23.29 miles per gallon of gas.

Math Review

279 ÷ 13.4 = ____	332 ÷ 24.2 = ____	(23,451 – 23,111) ÷ 16.9 = ____
359 ÷ 22.4 = ____	112 ÷ 5.2 = ____	(37,129 – 36,895) ÷ 9.8 = ____
471 ÷ 15.2 = ____	274 ÷ 8.1 = ____	(111,953 – 111,622) ÷ 13.7 = ____
579 ÷ 18.1 = ____	411 ÷ 14.3 = ____	(53,242 – 52,821) ÷ 12.6 = ____

MyFinLitLab **Apply Your Knowledge**

1. Iona drove 445 miles and it took 17.4 gallons to refill her tank. What is her MPG?

2. Barry's odometer on his car read 34,598 miles when he filled up his tank. The next time he refilled his tank, his odometer read 34,924 miles and it took 14.5 gallons to fill it up. What is his MPG?

3. Jonas drove 551 miles on a tank of gas in his new fuel-efficient vehicle. When he refilled his car it took 12.3 gallons to top off the tank. What is his MPG?

4. Jasmine put 16.4 gallons of gas in her car. She noted on her trip odometer that she had driven 431 miles on this tank of gas. What is her MPG?

5. Assume Jasmine wants to take a trip that will be about 2,000 miles in total and gas costs $3.75 a gallon. How much will she need to budget for her trip given her fuel efficiency you calculated in question 4?

Name: ____________________

Date: ____________________

Miscellaneous Financial Calculations

CONCEPT #4: Calculating Tips

Many restaurants that have waiters and waitresses anticipate you leaving a tip for good service. Tips are usually expressed as a percentage of the amount of your meal and commonly range from 15 percent and higher depending on the level of service. For example, you may have just eaten a nice meal that cost $40 and you want to leave a 15 percent tip. How much should you leave? $40 × .15 = $6.

Math Review

55 × .20 = _____	121 × .20 = _____	62 × .18 = _____
30 × .15 = _____	85 × .15 = _____	70 × .18 = _____
20 × .15 = _____	48 × .15 = _____	110 × .25 = _____
35 × .20 = _____	44 × .20 = _____	200 × .20 = _____

MyFinLitLab **Apply Your Knowledge**

1. Jerome just took his date to a nice restaurant, and the meal was $65. How much should he leave if he decides to tip 20 percent?

2. Marc was a waiter and the total tab at his last table was $211. How much should his tip have been if they left a 15 percent tip?

3. Kerri wanted to tip her waiter 20 percent for the meal because the service was really good. How much should she leave if the meal was $15.75?

4. Donna tipped the waitress 25 percent because the service was outstanding and it was a large party. If the total meal tab was $255, how much tip did she leave?

5. Peter tipped his waitress 20 percent on a meal that cost $75. How much tip did he leave?

Name: ______________________

Date: ______________________

CHAPTER 16

Miscellaneous Financial Calculations

OPEN RESPONSE #1

Please answer all parts of the question in the space provided.

Prompt: Abigail got her first paycheck. She wanted to save half of it and go shopping with the remaining money. This would be a good opportunity to buy clothes for work. Most of what she had was good for school, but she needed dressier clothes for the office where she had an internship.

One of the large department stores was having a storewide sale for clothing for fall at 40 percent off. She knew that she wanted a new pair of $52 pants, a couple of tops at $32 each to go with the pants, and an $89 jacket.

1. Explain to Abigail how to calculate the sales price for the merchandise.
2. Calculate what the sale price for each item Abigail has chosen will be and the total for her purchases. Show and explain how you got your answer.

Scoring Guide

4 Student gives correct answers for parts 1 and 2. All explanations are clear and complete. There is evidence of clear understanding of the concept.

3 Student gives correct answers for parts 1 and 2. Explanations are correct, but possibly unclear. There is less evidence of clear understanding.

2 Student answers 1 (1 or 2) part of the questions completely correct. There is some evidence of understanding.

1 Student gives only parts of correct answers. There is little evidence of understanding.

0 Response is totally incorrect or irrelevant (does not add any new information to the question).

Name: ______________________

Date: ______________________

Miscellaneous Financial Calculations

OPEN RESPONSE #2

Please answer all parts of the question in the space provided.

Prompt: Myles bought a used SUV. His father wants him to keep good records every time Myles fills the tank. Myles can budget for gas money better by knowing what the MPG is for his car.

After one month, Myles filled his gas tank. He recorded 16.2 gallons of gas for his SUV. The odometer read 27,895 miles when he purchased the car. This was his first fill up and the odometer read 28,267miles.

1. Explain to Myles how to calculate his miles per gallon (MPG).
2. Calculate the MPG for Myles. Show and explain how you got your answer.

Scoring Guide

4 Student gives correct answers for parts 1 and 2. All explanations are clear and complete. There is evidence of clear understanding of the concept.

3 Student gives correct answers for parts 1 and 2. Explanations are correct, but possibly unclear. There is less evidence of clear understanding.

2 Student answers 1 (1 or 2) part of the questions completely correct. There is some evidence of understanding.

1 Student gives only parts of correct answers. There is little evidence of understanding.

0 Response is totally incorrect or irrelevant (does not add any new information to the question).

Mortgages

There are a number of additional mortgage topics that are covered in more detail in this appendix. First, we will introduce some of the various types of mortgages you might encounter. We will then spend some time discussing some of the more common ratios lenders may use when evaluating loan applications. We also will provide a brief introduction to the appraisal process. And, lastly, we also will look at the various other up-front expenses you may incur when buying a home, such as origination fees, points, and appraisal fees.

Types of Mortgages

We learned how to calculate mortgage payments using the formula method in Chapter 15. That method will work to calculate any of the initial mortgage payments discussed here. However, the use of an Internet-based mortgage calculator will help us see the amount of interest and principal paid with each payment. Remember, each payment will reduce the principal slightly so that successive payments will have a smaller interest component and a larger principal reduction. In the early part of each loan, the largest fraction of a payment will be the interest component.

With this in mind, we will look at three types of mortgages: 1) fixed-rate mortgages, 2) adjustable-rate mortgages, and 3) balloon mortgages. We will use the terms *amortization* and *amortization table* in this discussion. Amortization is the process of paying a loan over a period of time. An amortization table shows us how much of each payment is allocated to paying accrued interest and how much is allocated toward reducing principal. Remember, for each payment these amounts will differ. Go to the following Web site to use their payment calculator. This site gives you the option of viewing the amortization table or amortization schedule.

http://www.amortization-calc.com/

Fixed-Rate Mortgages

Fixed-rate mortgages lock in the interest rate for the life of the loan. For example, if you have a $150,000, 30-year, 6 percent fixed-rate loan, you will always pay 6 percent interest on the outstanding balance for as long as you have the loan or until maturity. Using the calculator at the link above, you will find that the monthly payment will be $899.33 on this loan. At the end of 30 years you will have repaid the entire $150,000 loan. Note that you can see how much interest you will pay over some period of time.

Use this loan calculator to answer all of the following questions. Set the calculator to show results by the month.

Practice Questions

1. How much is the monthly payment on a $200,000 loan financed for 30 years at 6 percent?

2. How much interest will you pay in the first six months of this loan?

3. How much do you still owe on this loan after one year?

Adjustable-Rate Mortgages (ARMs)

Adjustable-rate mortgages remain fixed for some initial period and then adjust to reflect market interest rates. There are dozens of different ARMs, so we will simplify in order to illustrate the concept. For example, assume you have a $200,000 one-year ARM with a 6 percent initial rate that is a 30-year mortgage. A one-year ARM adjusts to market interest rates after a one-year period. This mortgage will be amortized just like a fixed rate for the initial period. Therefore, the initial payment will be identical to the payment calculated in the previous problem. It will be $1,199.10 per month. However, the interest rate on this mortgage will adjust after that first year. Let's assume it adjusts to 7 percent. How much will your new payment be? Refer to the previous problem. You now owe $197,544 and have 29 years remaining on your mortgage. Plug those numbers into the calculator and you see that the payment will be $1,327.75. Your house payment increased by $128.65 ($1,327.75 – $1,199.10 = $128.65). The interest rates on ARMs are tied to common market rates and adjust according to some formula determined when the mortgage was originated.

ARMs are often quoted as a 1/1 ARM, 3/1 ARM, or 5/1 ARM. The first number is the fixed-rate period. The second number is the frequency of adjustment. For example, a 3/1 ARM will be fixed for the first three years and will adjust every year after that according to the formula spelled out at origination. Most ARMs are capped in the total amount they can adjust over the life of the loan or at any one adjustment period.

Practice Questions

1. How much will the new payment be on a $150,000, 30-year, 6 percent 3/1 ARM that adjusts to an 8 percent rate after three years? (It will help to set the calculator to show results by year.)

2. Using the same data, how much would the payment be if the interest rate adjusted to 7 percent instead?

3. Using the information from the previous question, how much of payment number 37 is interest and how much will go toward principal reduction?

Balloon Mortgages

Balloon mortgages are mortgages that are amortized over a longer period, but in which the entire loan balance becomes due earlier. For example, you may have a 5-year balloon mortgage that is amortized over a 30-year period. That is, your payments for those five years are made as if you were paying the loan off over 30 years. But at the end of the five years, the entire loan balance is due. This amount is often refinanced at this time. Common balloon periods are three, five, and seven years. People sometimes choose balloon payments because the interest rates are typically lower than a comparable fixed-rate mortgage or ARM. If you intend to move in the five to seven years, balloon mortgages often can be a viable option.

For example, using the data from Practice Question 2 at the bottom of page 172, the balloon payment after three years would be $144,126.11. If housing values fall, then balloon mortgages can be problematic. You might not be able to finance the full amount you owe if the value of the mortgaged property has declined in value.

Practice Questions

1. How much is the balloon payment on a 5-year $170,000 balloon mortgage financed at 6 percent using a 30-year amortization?

2. How much is the balloon payment on a 3-year $130,000 balloon mortgage financed at 9 percent using a 30-year amortization?

3. How much is the balloon payment on a 7-year $200,000 balloon mortgage financed at 5 percent using a 30-year amortization?

Ratios

There are a number of ratios used in the lending industry to determine how much money a person can borrow and ultimately repay. Let's look at a few of the more common ratios used when you are trying to get a home mortgage.

Debt-to-Income Ratios

Debt-to-income ratios measure a borrower's ability to meet his or her monthly debt obligations and are expressed as a percentage. There are two main types of debt-to-income ratios: 1) front-end ratio and 2) back-end ratio. We will discuss each one. In each case, a lower ratio is always better from a lender's perspective. A lower ratio means it takes a smaller fraction of your income to make your payments.

1) Front-End Ratio

Lenders use the front-end ratio as a measure of someone's ability to make monthly housing payments. This ratio identifies the fraction of a person's (or household's) income that will be needed for housing expenses. It is calculated by the following formula:

Front-end ratio = Monthly housing expenses/gross monthly income

The monthly housing expenses are commonly known as PITI. PITI is an acronym for principal, interest, taxes, and insurance. In many cases your monthly house payment will include each of these four components. The bank or mortgage company will collect all this money and distribute it to the proper recipient. In other cases, your payment may only include the principal and interest, and you will be billed separately for real estate taxes and insurance. In either case, however, the monthly housing expenses will include all four components.

Calculating gross monthly income simply involves taking your annual income before tax and converting that to a monthly amount by dividing by 12 months.

In practice, lenders establish a front-end ratio that they will not allow any potential borrower to exceed. This ratio typically ranges between 25–35 percent. For example, if a lender requires your front-end ratio to be 28 percent or lower and your gross income is $48,000 a year, then you can calculate the maximum monthly housing expense you can afford. Your total monthly housing expense cannot exceed 28 percent of your monthly income which is ($48,000 ÷ 12)(.28) = $1,120. Your front end ratio would be $1,120 ÷ $4,000 = .28 or 28 percent. As long as your PITI did not exceed $1,120 per month you would be eligible for the loan using this criterion.

Practice Questions

1. How much total monthly housing expense can you afford if the lender requires your maximum front-end ratio to be no more than 28 percent and you earn $65,000 per year?

2. How much total monthly housing expense can you afford if the lender requires your maximum front-end ratio to be no more than 31 percent and you earn $42,000 per year?

3. How much total monthly housing expense can you afford if the lender requires your maximum front-end ratio to be no more than 26 percent and you earn $105,000 per year?

2) Back-End Ratio

The back-end ratio is calculated in the same manner as the front-end ratio with one exception. The numerator now adds other monthly debt payments to the monthly housing PITI payments. This ratio tells lenders just how much debt you have relative to your income level. Obviously, the lower this ratio, the more likely you will be to repay your debts.

Back-end ratio = Total monthly debt service/gross monthly income

For example, maybe you have a gross monthly income of $5,000 and a monthly car payment of $550. Assuming your back-end ratio cannot exceed 36 percent, how much could your house payment be if the car note was your only debt? Set X = to your house payment and solve for X.

($550 + X) ÷ $5,000 = .36
$550 + X = $5,000 × .36
$550 + X = $1,800
X = $1,800 – $550
X = $1,250

So, your PITI could not exceed $1,250 using the back-end ratio requirement of this lender. Note that you also would need to satisfy the lender's front-end ratio.

Practice Questions

1. If your annual income is $48,000 and you have a $276 car payment, what is the maximum amount your total monthly housing expense can be if the lender uses a maximum of 38 percent for the back-end ratio?

2. If your annual income is $64,000 and you have a $621 car payment, what is the maximum amount your total monthly housing expense can be if the lender uses a maximum of 41 percent for the back-end ratio?

3. If your annual income is $81,000 and you have one car payment of $435 a month and another car payment of $338 a month, what is the maximum amount your total monthly housing expense can be if the lender uses a maximum of 36 percent for the back-end ratio?

Loan-to-Value Ratio (LTV)

Lenders commonly use loan-to-value (LTV) ratios to establish a maximum amount they are willing to lend on a specific house or other asset. In general, lenders would like to see a lower LTV. A lower ratio means the borrower has more of his or her own money tied up in the asset and so has a lower likelihood of default. For example, if a house is appraised for $100,000 and a lender uses an LTV of 80 percent, or .80, the lender will only loan $80,000 on that house ($100,000 × .80 = $80,000). The lower LTV ratio ensures that the borrower has some equity in the property and a reason to want to continue making payments. In this case, the borrower has a $20,000 investment in the house and will be more likely to make payments. The borrower will know that if he or she defaults, he or she will lose the $20,000. LTVs are calculated in the following manner:

Loan-to-value ratio = loan amount ÷ appraised value of the property

Let's look at one more example. Assume you are buying a house appraised at $200,000 and the lender uses a 90 percent LTV ratio. How much will they loan on the house?

$$\$200,000 \times .90 = \$180,000$$

This means that the borrower must come up with the difference of $20,000, which is also called a down payment.

We will address the methods of real estate appraisals later in this appendix. For now, understand that an appraisal is the process of an independent expert determining a market value for an asset such as real estate.

Practice Questions

1. Assume you are buying a house appraised at $145,000 and the lender uses a 95 percent LTV ratio. How much will they loan on the house?

2. Assume you are buying a house appraised at $275,000 and the lender uses an 85 percent LTV ratio. How much will they loan on the house?

3. Assume you are buying a house appraised at $80,000 that you intend to use for a rental property. For rentals, the lender uses a 70 percent LTV ratio. How much money will you have to come up with for a down payment?

Combined-Loan-to-Value Ratio (CLTV)

Lenders use the combined-loan-to-value ratios in the exact same manner they use the LTV ratio, except that the CLTV is used when a borrower takes out a second mortgage on a property. Second mortgages are sometimes used at purchase with a first mortgage of 80 percent LTV and a second, higher interest rate mortgage from a different lender used to finance a portion of the 20 percent down payment. A home equity loan also is an example of a second mortgage.

$$\text{Combined-loan-to-value ratio} = \frac{\text{total loan amount of first and second mortgage}}{\text{appraised value of the property}}$$

For example, assume you are buying a house appraised for $160,000. You may find a lender willing to loan you $120,000 using a first mortgage. Another lender has agreed to loan you $20,000 at a higher interest rate using a second mortgage. What is your combined-loan-to-value ratio?

$$\text{CLTV} = (\$120,000 + \$20,000) \div \$160,000 = .875 \text{ or } 87.5 \text{ percent}$$

Practice Questions

1. What is the CLTV of a property appraised for $220,000 that has a first mortgage of $140,000 and another mortgage of $32,000?

2. What is the CLTV of a property appraised for $145,000 that has a first mortgage of $100,000 and another mortgage of $25,000?

3. What is the CLTV of a property appraised for $207,000 that has a first mortgage of $160,000 and another mortgage of $24,000?

Real Property Appraisal Methods

Since we have used real estate appraisal values throughout this appendix, we need to address the way appraisals are determined. You can see the importance of the appraisal since the appraised value determines the amount you will be allowed to borrow on a specific house or piece of real estate. There are three primary methods used to determine property value. They are 1) sales comparisons of comparables, 2) replacement cost approach, and 3) income approach.

1) Sales Comparisons of Comparables

This method is used most often in residential real estate. A qualified real estate appraiser will access a database of recent sales for properties that are similar to the one being appraised. The comparable properties will be in close geographic proximity, usually within 3 to 5 miles, of the property being appraised. An appraiser will commonly use three comparables.

Using the sales price as a base, the appraiser will then make adjustments to the property being appraised. The appraiser will add value if the house has additional features the comparables did not have. The appraiser will also subtract value if the property being appraised does not have some feature the other properties did have. For example, maybe the house being appraised has a fireplace, but the back yard is not fenced. The three comparables may have fences but not fireplaces. The appraiser will add value to the appraised home for the fireplace and subtract value for the lack of a fence. The adjustment values are to some degree subject to the appraiser's own judgment and depend on the local sales data. After all adjustments have been made, the appraiser will determine a fair market value for the property. This method works well when there have been recent sales near the house being appraised.

Simplified example: The three comparables sold for an average of $137,500 each. However, the home being appraised has a fireplace (+$2,000), a fenced back yard (+$3,000), but only a single-car garage instead of a two-car garage (–$6,000). Using these numbers, the value of the property being appraised would be $137,500 + $2,000 + $3,000 – $6,000 = $136,500. In reality this is an extremely complex process and has been simplified for this example. For one, average values of comparables are not used.

2) Replacement Cost Approach

Appraisers may use this method for properties for which there are few or no comparable sales. The appraiser calculates the square footage of the home and multiplies that amount by the per-square-foot-cost of building similar properties. That value is adjusted by deducting any depreciation of the property. For example, the house or structure may be 30 years old and need repairs. The depreciation component will adjust the value down because of this fact. Finally, the value of the land is added in to the total appraised value.

Simplified example: New construction in the region costs $125 a square foot. What is the value of a 2,200-square-foot home that has a total of $35,000 in depreciated value if the land is worth about $50,000?

$$(2{,}200 \times \$125) - \$35{,}000 + \$50{,}000 = \$290{,}000$$

3) Income Approach

Apprasiers use this method for income-generating properties such as rentals. The appraiser first estimates the expected gross income or financial benefit from the property and treats that as an annual cash flow. Then the appraiser calculates the present value of that cash flow using the interest rate that the owner is expecting to earn on that investment.

So, consider this example: The appraiser estimates the property will generate $12,000 a year in cash flows from rents and tax breaks. The owner is hoping for a return on his or her investment equal to an annual rate of 8 percent. What is the value of this property if the cash flows are forecast to continue for 20 years? Note that this is an annuity, so you can use:

$12,000 PMT
8 INT
20 N
CPT PV = $117,817.77

All of these examples have been greatly simplified to illustrate the general concepts of appraisal. In reality, real property appraisals are a complex process. Ask a licensed appraiser to visit your class to go over some of the details involved in an appraisal in your area.

Practice Questions

1. Using the sales comparison approach, what is the value of a house where the average value of the comparables was $176,300? The appraiser will also add $8,000 for an extra room above the garage and subtract $3,000 for the lack of a fenced yard.

2. Using the replacement cost approach, how much is an 1,800-square-foot house worth that has about $44,000 in depreciation adjustments and a land value of $67,500 if the cost of new construction is $210 a square foot?

3. Using the income approach, what is the value of a rental property that you expect will generate $8,400 a year in positive cash flows for another 15 years if you want to earn a 7 percent rate of return?

Up-Front Expenses

Whenever you borrow money to buy a home, there are numerous fees you may have to pay. These fees include origination fees, appraisal fees, prorated taxes or other expenses, private mortgage insurance (PMI), and points to buy a lower interest rate.

Origination Fees The mortgage originator will do the paperwork for your mortgage, but will charge an origination fee for this process. This fee can range from several hundred dollars to several thousand dollars. It often depends on the total amount of the loan, the mortgage company policy, the quality of the borrower's credit, and other factors. Shop around, since origination fees vary widely.

Appraisal Fees Lenders often use an independent and licensed real estate appraiser to determine the value of a house or piece of property. Appraisers typically charge from $300 to $500 for a residential appraisal. They are essentially determining a market value for the property.

Prorated Fees To prorate something is to divide into portions. Taxes are the most common prorated fee. Property tax is paid on an annual basis for the previous year. So, if you sell a property in the middle of a tax year, you may owe a portion of the upcoming property tax bill. The process of bringing the property bill current at the time of sale is called prorating. Let's assume the annual property tax on a house is $1,200 per year. If you sell the home 5 months into the tax year, you will need to pay 5/12 of the taxes at closing. Closing is the process of completing the legal paperwork for a real estate transaction. So, 5/12 of $1,200 = $500.

Points Borrowers may opt to pay points on a mortgage to buy their interest rate down. One point is equal to one percent of the loan amount. For example, one point on a $200,000 loan is equal to $2,000. Paying points will cause a reduction in your interest rate and subsequently your payment. However, the amount of the reduction varies from lender to lender and depends on a number of market factors. Sometimes points may be a good deal, other times they are not.

Private Mortgage Insurance, or PMI Lenders require private mortgage insurance on many loans when the LTV exceeds 80 percent. Companies sell PMI to mortgage originators on loans so that if the borrower defaults, the PMI will repay the top 20 percent of the loan. The lender then hopes it will recover the remaining amount upon repossession and sale of the mortgaged property. PMI is charged to the borrower and included in the monthly house payment. The use of PMI allows some borrowers to obtain a mortgage with a very low down payment since the default risk is now shifted to the insurance company. The amount of PMI depends on the total amount of the mortgage, but can range from a few hundred to over a thousand dollars a year. Lenders are required by law to cancel PMI when the LTV on the loan falls below 78 percent.

Other Fees It is also common to see home inspection fees, pest control inspection fees, and various other fees. These can include recording fees to record the legal transfer of property at the courthouse, and title insurance to make sure the legal title is free of any defects that could cause financial problems for the new owner.

Example

In most cases these fees are rolled into the amount of the mortgage if the borrowers opt to do so. Let's look at a comprehensive example. Assume you are evaluating a $180,000 30-year fixed-rate mortgage. The fees follow:

Origination fee	$800
Prorated taxes	$1,500
Appraisal fee	$500
Other fees	$400
Total	$3,200

PMI will cost $100 per month and the borrower has the option of paying 7 percent interest or 6.8 percent interest with one point. Evaluate these options assuming all fees will be financed into the loan.

The loan amount without points will be $180,000 + $3,200 = $183,200. Using the mortgage calculator, you find the payment for this amount for 30 years at 7 percent interest is $1,218.83 + $100 in PMI = $1,318.83.

If you choose to buy the interest rate down, you will pay 1 percent of the loan amount of $183,200 = $1,832 in points. Again, assume you will finance the points into the mortgage. (While this would actually increase the points slightly, we will ignore this minor difference for simplicity.) This loan would be $183,200 + $1,832 = $185,032 financed for 30 years at 6.8 percent interest. The payment would be $1,206.27 + $100 PMI = $1,306.27.

While paying points makes the payment lower by a few dollars per month, it might not be a good investment unless you plan on living in the home for 30 years. Otherwise, you might not recover the $1,832 that you paid in points.

Practice Question

1. Assume you are evaluating a $120,000 30-year fixed-rate mortgage. The fees are as follows:

Origination fee	$1,100
Pro-rated taxes	$1,600
Appraisal fee	$400
Other fees	$500
Total	$3,600

PMI will cost $70 per month. The borrower has the option of paying 8 percent interest or can pay one point and buy the interest rate down to 7.5 percent. Evaluate these options assuming all fees will be financed into the loan.

Supply and Demand

In a free market, supply and demand are forces that determine prices. Supply and demand analysis is a complex topic, but a simplified presentation may help you understand how and why prices change in a competitive market.

In the United States, competitive markets surround us. Almost everything we buy is subject to competitive forces. With this in mind, it is easy to understand supply and demand and the pressures they put on prices. Think about it like this: What if you were able to buy T-shirts for $10 and then able to turn around and sell them at a local flea market for $20? Ignoring all other costs you would make a $10 per shirt profit ($20 – $10 = $10 profit). What would happen if you told your friend about this wonderful opportunity? She also buys some T-shirts for $10 and opens another booth at the flea market. But now, with the two of you selling the same product for $20, there are too many T-shirts for sale. There simply aren't enough buyers interested in T-shirts at the $20 price. Your friend is disappointed, so she decides to sell them at $18 each to undercut your price. Now all the buyers flock to your friend's booth to purchase your friend's shirts. Faced with dropping sales, you might respond by lowering your price to $16, and so on.

What's happening here? Well, for one you have a new definition of friend. But, secondly, you can see how the competition between you two is forcing prices down. This would likely continue until you reached a point where you would attract enough buyers so that you could both sell T-shirts and make a profit. Or, perhaps you would reach the point where you would be unwilling to go any lower—and one of you might leave the business.

Notice that there are two sides to this equation. You are *supplying* the T-shirts. Your customers are *demanding* the T-shirts. It is the interaction of both supply and demand that will determine price. This relationship between supply, demand, and price can be expressed graphically. With a graph, you can see what happens to price when we change either supply or demand. For example, the supply changed in the previous example because new sellers (suppliers) entered the market.

Let's look at this relationship graphically. We can create what is called a demand curve for T-shirts from the following demand schedule. This is simply a table that lists the numbers of T-shirts our customers would demand—that is, be willing to buy—at each price.

Price	Quantity Demanded
$20	20
$18	25
$16	30
$14	35
$12	40

We will plot these pairs of points on a graph, with price on the vertical axis and quantity demanded (Q) on the horizontal axis. Also note that as we lower price, consumers are willing and able to purchase more T-shirts. This law of demand holds true for most products: as price falls, quantity demanded goes up.

When you plot these points and connect the dots, you see a typical demand curve that is downward sloping and to the right.

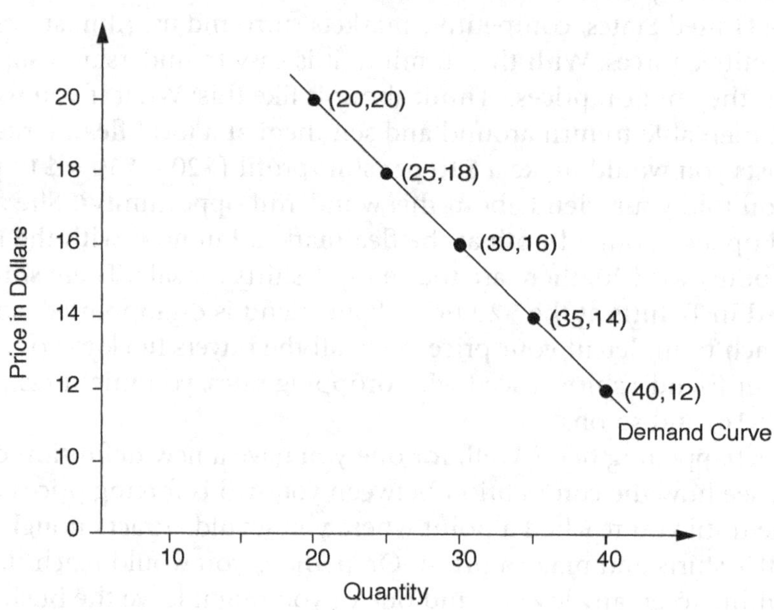

Supply is the opposite of demand. As price increases, suppliers are willing and able to supply more T-shirts. The higher profits attract more sellers and cause existing sellers to want to sell more units.

Let's look at this relationship graphically. We can create a supply curve for T-shirts from the following supply schedule. This is simply a table that lists the numbers of T-shirts we would be willing to supply or sell at each price. Notice that these numbers are directly related. As price increases, so does quantity supplied.

Price	Quantity Supplied
$20	40
$18	35
$16	30
$14	25
$12	20

Notice in the following graph that the supply curve is upward sloping and to the right. This is the typical shape of the supply curve. Also notice that the pair of points where the supply and demand intersect is at a price of $16 per shirt, and 30 shirts will be sold at this price. This point is known as the equilibrium, or market clearing point.

T-Shirt Market

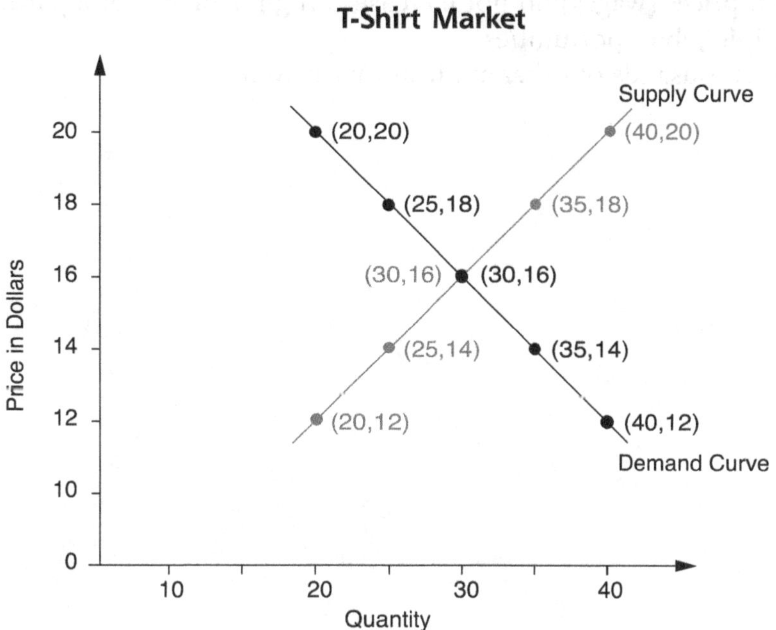

What can we learn from this analysis? Understanding the impact of changes in demand or supply can help us predict the direction of prices of many goods and services. For example, an increase in demand would mean that at every price level there are more units demanded of a product. For example, suppose our T-shirts became a hot fashion trend and suddenly everyone had to have one or two. This would be an increase in demand, or a shift to the right, as shown below. Note that price will be higher at the new equilibrium point, and more units will be sold. If demand were to shift to the left, price and quantity would fall. Supply shifts—for example, from the shutdown of a factory or the addition of new sellers to a market—would generate higher or lower prices as well.

T-Shirt Market

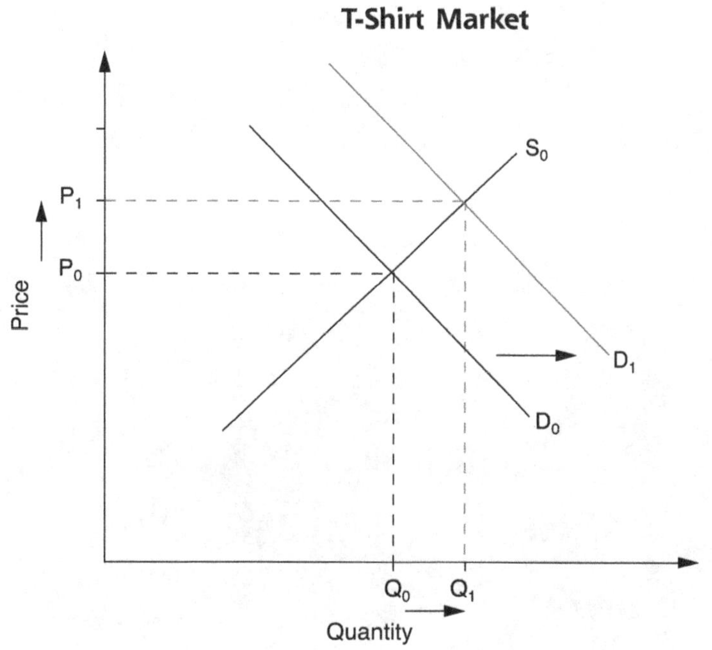

How could you apply this knowledge in your financial life? What if you thought that the demand for health-care services (nurses, doctors, and so on) would be higher due to the aging of Americans? What would you expect to happen to the prices paid for these services? Prices (wages) should increase as a result. This thought might make you decide on a career in health care. Even if prices (wages) do not increase, a high demand for a particular skill set can guarantee multiple job opportunities.

There are thousands of other applications as well.

DOE 8

DOE 8